BLACK&DECKER®
HOME IMPROVEMENT LIBRARY™

Advanced Home Wiring

CREATIVE PUBLISHING international

MINNETONKA, MINNESOTA

Contents

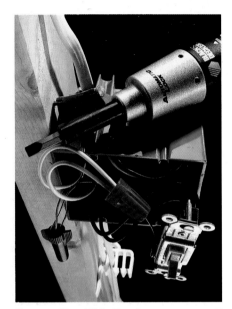

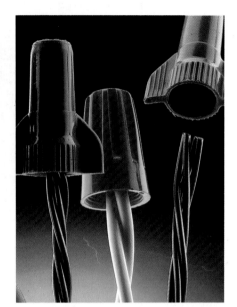

Copyright © 1992
Creative Publishing international, Inc.
5900 Green Oak Drive
Minnetonka, Minnesota 55343
1-800-328-3895
All rights reserved
Printed in U.S.A.

Books available in this series:
Everyday Home Repairs, Decorating With Paint & Wallcovering, Carpentry: Tools • Shelves • Walls • Doors, Kitchen Remodeling, Building Decks, Home Plumbing Projects & Repairs, Basic Wiring & Electrical Repairs, Workshop Tips & Techniques, Advanced Home Wiring, Carpentry: Remodeling, Landscape Design & Construction, Bathroom Remodeling, Built-In Projects for the Home, Kitchen & Bathroom Ideas, Refinishing & Finishing Wood, Exterior Home Repairs & Improvements, Home Masonry Repairs & Projects, Building Porches & Patios, Deck & Landscape Ideas, Flooring Projects & Techniques, Advanced Deck Building, Advanced Home Plumbing, Complete Guide to Home Wiring, Complete Guide to Home Plumbing

Library of Congress
Cataloging-in-Publication Data

Advanced home wiring.

p. cm.—(Black & Decker home improvement library)
Includes index.
ISBN 0-86573-718-5 (hardcover).
ISBN 0-86573-719-3 (softcover).
1. Electric Wiring, Interior—Amateurs' manuals. I. Cy DeCosse Incorporated. II. Series.
TK9901.A34 1992   91-37337
621.319'24—dc20

President: Iain Macfarlane

ADVANCED HOME WIRING
Created by: The Editors of Creative Publishing international, Inc., in cooperation with Black & Decker.
BLACK&DECKER is a trademark of the Black & Decker Corporation, and is used under license.

"Wire-Nut®" is a registered trademark of Ideal Industries, Inc.

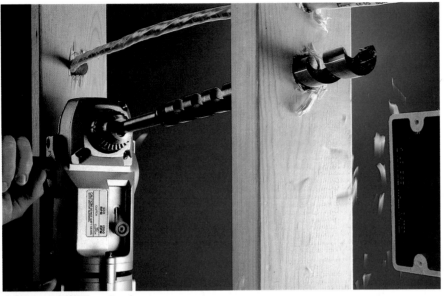

Advanced Wiring Projects 65

Managing Editor: Paul Currie
Senior Art Director: Tim Himsel
Editor: Bryan Trandem
Project Managers: Carol Harvatin,
  Dianne Talmage
Copy Editors: Tom Carpenter, Janice
  Cauley, Dick Sternberg
Art Director: Dave Schelitzche
*Director of Development Planning &
  Production:* Jim Bindas
Production Manager: Amelia Merz
Shop Supervisor: Greg Wallace
Photo Directors: Jim Huntley,
  Christopher Wilson
Set Builders: Jerry Blaze, Jim Huntley,
  Terry Petron, Wayne Wendland,
  Dan Zitzloff

Production Staff: Joe Fahey, Kevin D.
  Frakes, Peter Gloege, Melissa Grabanski,
  Jeff Hickman, Mark Jacobson, Daniel
  Meyers, Linda Schloegel, Nik Wogstad
Studio Managers: Cathleen Shannon,
  Rebecca Boyle
Assistant Studio Manager: Rena Tassone
Lead Photographers: John Lauenstein,
  Mike Parker
Photographers: Rex Irmen, Mark
  Macemon, Mette Nielsen, Cathleen
  Shannon, Phil Aarrestad, Kim Bailey,
  Dave Brus, Chuck Nields
Contributing Writers & Editors:
  Greg Breining, Al Hildenbrand
  (Al's Electric Works), Marty Kumm,
  Robert Weaver (Weaver Electric)

Contributing Manufacturers:
  Cooper Industries; Dicon Systems, Inc.;
  Encon Industries, Inc.; Gemini Industries,
  Inc.; Intellectron Inc.; L.E. Mason Co.;
  Nautilus; Nutone; Reiker Enterprises, Inc.;
  Sonin, Inc.; 3M (Electrical Products
  Division); Waxman Industries, Inc.

Printed on American paper by:
R.R. Donnelley & Sons Co.
10 9 8 7 6

3

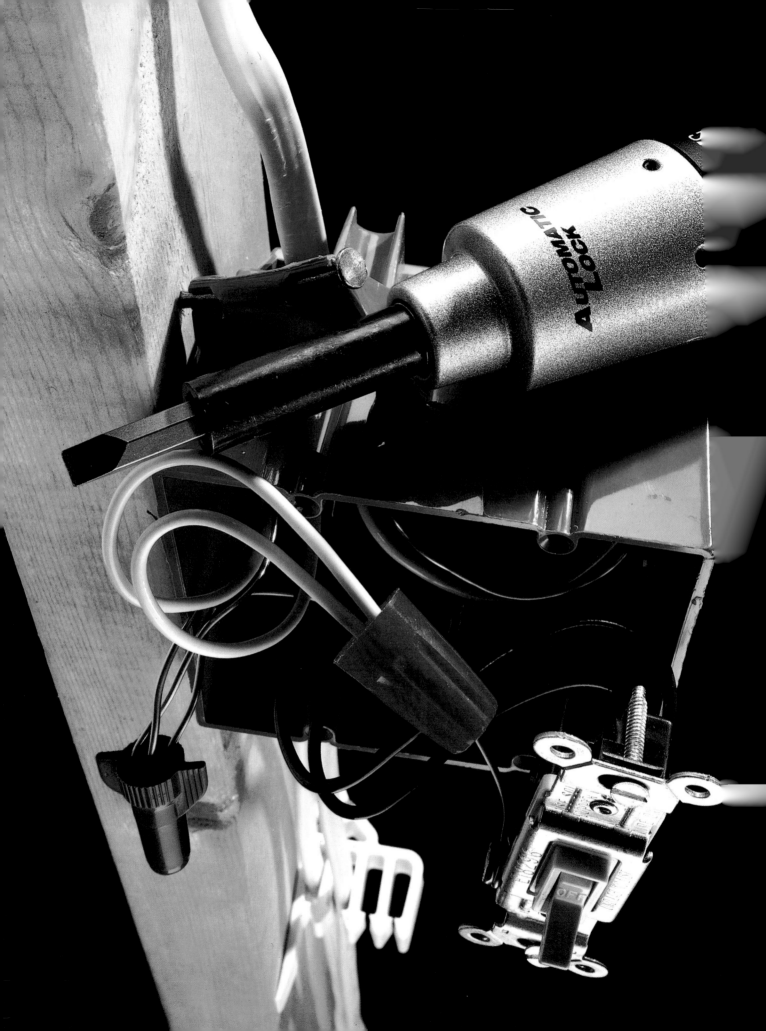

How to Use This Book

There is a great deal of satisfaction in doing your own electrical work. You will understand exactly how your house is wired, the principles behind the wiring, and your electrical power needs and capacities. You also will save a lot of money. *Advanced Home Wiring* shows the essential information for installing new wiring in your home remodeling projects, from planning through the final inspection.

First, you learn about "Planning a Wiring Project." You find out which Electrical Code requirements apply to your project, as well as how to work with your local electrical inspector. You see how to evaluate your existing electrical capacity and power usage, and determine the needs of the circuits you are adding. You also learn a step-by-step method for drawing a wiring diagram. A series of circuit maps shows you the most common wiring layouts to help you draw your diagram.

Next, in the section on "Tools, Materials & Techniques," learn about the tools and materials used in common wiring projects. You also find the general techniques for installing wiring in these projects.

Finally, three major wiring projects demonstrate the methods and techniques presented in the first two sections. "Wiring a Room Addition" presents information that applies to any addition, whether it is an attic or basement renovation, or a new room added on to your existing house. In "Wiring a Remodeled Kitchen" you find how to wire a kitchen or any other room using a lot of power and containing many specialty circuits. "Installing Outdoor Wiring" shows you how to get power to any outdoor location. Each project includes scale drawings to help you follow the projects from the planning stage through the final connections.

Advanced Home Wiring takes the mystery out of installing new circuits. This is a useful manual for your reference shelf and job site, combining thorough information with helpful step-by-step photos.

To get the most from *Advanced Home Wiring*, you should have an understanding of basic home wiring and electrical materials. You will find this information in *Basic Wiring & Electrical Repairs*, from the Black & Decker® Home Improvement Library™.

1. Examine your main service (page 8). The amp rating of the electrical service and the size of the circuit breaker panel will help you determine if a service upgrade is needed.

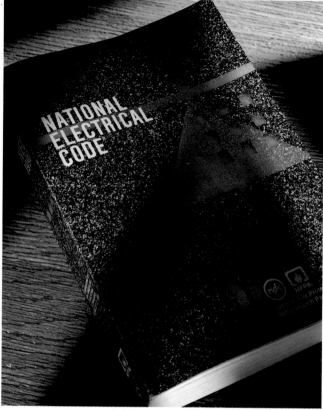

2. Learn about codes (pages 9 to 11). The National Electrical Code, and local Electrical Codes and Building Codes, provide guidelines for determining how much power and how many circuits your home needs. Your local electrical inspector can tell you which regulations apply to your job.

Planning a Wiring Project

Careful planning of a wiring project ensures you will have plenty of power for present and future needs. Whether you are adding circuits in a room addition, wiring a remodeled kitchen, or adding an outdoor circuit, consider all possible ways the space might be used, and plan for enough electrical service to meet peak needs.

For example, when wiring a room addition, remember that the way a room is used can change. In a room used as a spare bedroom, a single 15-amp circuit provides plenty of power, but if you ever choose to convert the same room to a family recreation space, it will need at least two 20-amp circuits.

When wiring a remodeled kitchen, it is a good idea to install circuits for an electric oven and countertop range, even if you do not have these electric appliances. Installing these circuits now makes it easy to convert from gas to electric appliances at a later date.

A large wiring project adds a considerable load to your main electrical service. In about 25% of all homes, some type of service upgrade is needed before new wiring can be installed. For example, many homeowners will need to replace an older 60-amp electrical service with a new service rated for 100 amps or more. This is a job for a licensed electrician, but is well worth the investment. In other cases, the existing main service provides adequate power, but the main circuit breaker panel is too full to hold any new circuit breakers. In this case, it is necessary to install a circuit breaker subpanel to provide room for hooking up added circuits. Installing a subpanel is a job most homeowners can do themselves (pages 60 to 63).

This chapter gives an easy five-step method for determining your electrical needs and planning new circuits.

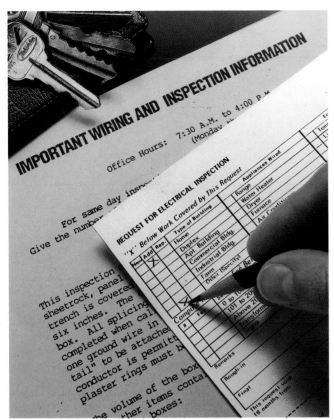

3. Prepare for inspections (pages 12 to 13). Remember that your work must be reviewed by your local electrical inspector. When planning your wiring project, always follow the inspector's guidelines for quality workmanship.

4. Evaluate electrical loads (pages 14 to 17). New circuits put an added load on your electrical service. Make sure the total load of the existing wiring and the planned new circuits does not exceed the main service capacity.

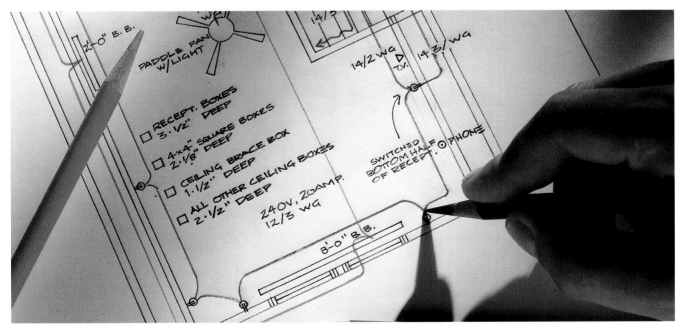

5. Draw a wiring diagram and get a permit (pages 18 to 19). Your inspector needs to see an accurate wiring diagram and materials list before he will issue a work permit for your project. This wiring plan also helps you organize your work.

1: Examine Your Main Service

The first step in planning a new wiring project is to look in your main circuit breaker panel and find the size of the service by reading the amperage rating on the main circuit breaker. As you plan new circuits and evaluate electrical loads, knowing the size of the main service helps you determine if you need a service upgrade.

Also look for open circuit breaker slots in the panel. The number of open slots will determine if you need to add a circuit breaker subpanel.

Find the service size by opening the main service panel and reading the amp rating printed on the main circuit breaker. In most cases, 100-amp service provides enough power to handle the added loads of projects like the ones shown in this book. A service rated for 60 amps or less may need to be upgraded.

Older service panels use fuses instead of circuit breakers. Have an electrician replace this type of panel with a circuit breaker panel that provides enough power and enough open breaker slots for the new circuits you are planning.

Circuit breaker panel with empty slots

Circuit breaker panel with no empty slots

Look for open circuit breaker slots in the main circuit breaker panel, or in a circuit breaker subpanel, if your home already has one. You will need one open slot for each 120-volt circuit you plan to install, and two

slots for each 240-volt circuit. If your main circuit breaker panel has no open breaker slots, install a subpanel (pages 60 to 63) to provide room for connecting new circuits.

2: Learn about Codes

To ensure public safety, your community requires that you get a permit to install new wiring and have the completed work reviewed by an appointed inspector. Electrical inspectors use the National Electrical Code (NEC) as the primary authority for evaluating wiring, but they also follow the local Building Code and Electrical Code standards.

As you begin planning new circuits, call or visit your local electrical inspector and discuss the project with him. The inspector can tell you which of the national and local Code requirements apply to your job, and may give you a packet of information summarizing these regulations. Later, when you apply to the inspector for a work permit, he will expect you to understand the local guidelines as well as a few basic National Electrical Code requirements.

The National Electrical Code is a set of standards that provides minimum safety requirements for wiring installations. It is revised every three years. The national Code requirements for the projects shown in this book are thoroughly explained on the following pages. For more information, you can find copies of the current NEC, as well as a number of excellent handbooks based on the NEC, at libraries and bookstores.

In addition to being the final authority on Code requirements, inspectors are electrical professionals with years of experience. Although they have busy schedules, most inspectors are happy to answer questions and help you design well-planned circuits.

Basic Electrical Code Requirements

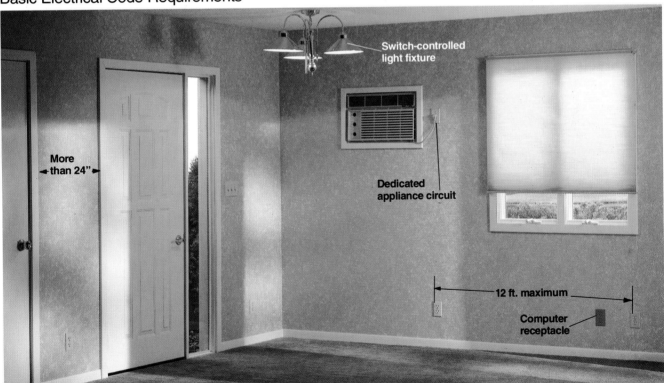

Electrical Code requirements for living areas:
Living areas need at least one 15-amp or 20-amp basic lighting/receptacle circuit for each 600 square feet of living space, and should have a "dedicated" circuit for each type of permanent appliance, like an air conditioner, computer, or a group of baseboard heaters. Receptacles on basic lighting/receptacle circuits should be spaced no more than 12 ft. apart. Many electricians and electrical inspectors recommend even closer spacing. Any wall more than 24" wide also needs a receptacle. Every room should have a wall switch at the point of entry to control either a ceiling light or plug-in lamp. Kitchens and bathrooms must have a ceiling-mounted light fixture.

(continued next page)

Measure the living areas of your home, excluding closets and unfinished spaces. A sonic measuring tool gives room dimensions quickly, and contains a built-in calculator for figuring floor area. You will need a minimum of one basic lighting/receptacle circuit for every 600 sq. ft. of living space. The total square footage also helps you determine heating and cooling needs for new room additions (page 13).

Stairways with six steps or more must have lighting that illuminates each step. The light fixture must be controlled by three-way switches at the top and bottom landings.

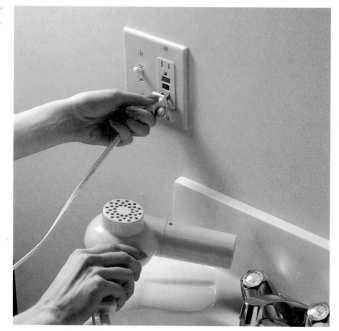

Kitchen and bathroom receptacles must be protected by a ground-fault circuit-interrupter (GFCI). Also, all outdoor receptacles and general-use receptacles in an unfinished basement or crawl space must be protected by a GFCI.

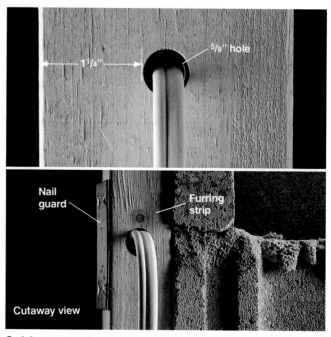

Cables must be protected against damage by nails and screws by at least 1¹/4" of wood (top). When cables pass through 2 × 2 furring strips (bottom), protect the cables with metal nail guards.

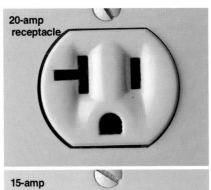

Closets and other storage spaces need at least one light fixture that is controlled by a wall switch near the entrance. Prevent fire hazards by positioning the light fixtures so the outer globes are at least 12" away from all shelf areas.

Hallways more than 10 ft. long need at least one receptacle. All hallways should have a switch-controlled light fixture.

Amp ratings of receptacles must match the size of the circuit. A common mistake is to use 20-amp receptacles (top) on 15-amp circuits—a potential cause of dangerous circuit overloads.

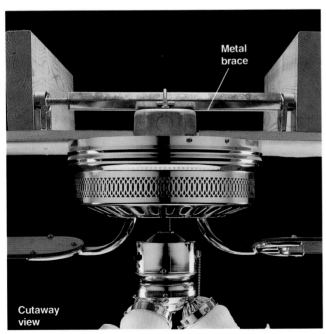

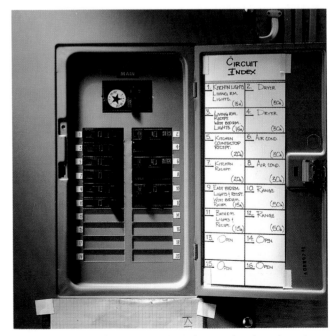

A metal brace attached to framing members is required for ceiling fans and large light fixtures that are too heavy to be supported by an electrical box.

Label new circuits on an index attached to the circuit breaker panel. List the rooms and appliances controlled by each circuit. Make sure the area around the panel is clean, well lighted, and accessible.

3: Prepare for Inspections

The electrical inspector who issues the work permit for your wiring project will also visit your home to review the work. Make sure to allow time for these inspections as you plan the project. For most projects, an inspector makes two visits.

The first inspection, called the "rough-in," is done after the cables are run between the boxes, but before the insulation, wallboard, switches, and fixtures are installed. The second inspection, called the "final," is done after the walls and ceilings are finished and all electrical connections are made.

When preparing for the rough-in inspection, make sure the area is neat. Sweep up sawdust and clean up any pieces of scrap wire or cable insulation. Before inspecting the boxes and cables, the inspector will check to make sure all plumbing and other mechanical work is completed. Some electrical inspectors will ask to see your building and plumbing permits.

At the final inspection, the inspector checks random boxes to make sure the wire connections are correct. If he sees good workmanship at the selected boxes, the inspection will be over quickly. However, if he spots a problem, the inspector may choose to inspect every connection.

Inspectors have busy schedules, so it is a good idea to arrange for an inspection several days or weeks in advance. In addition to basic compliance with Code, the inspector wants your work to meet his own standards for workmanship. When you apply for a work permit, make sure you understand what the inspector will look for during inspections.

You cannot put new circuits into use legally until the inspector approves them at the final inspection. Because the inspector is responsible for the safety of all wiring installations, his approval means that your work meets professional standards. If you have planned carefully and done your work well, electrical inspections are routine visits that give you confidence in your own skills.

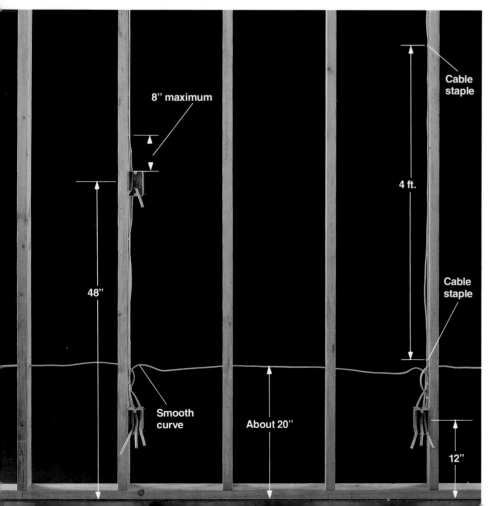

8" maximum

48"

Smooth curve

About 20"

Cable staple

4 ft.

Cable staple

12"

Inspectors measure to see that electrical boxes are mounted at consistent heights. Measured from the center of the boxes, receptacles in living areas typically are located 12" above the finished floor, and switches at 48". For special circumstances, inspectors allow you to alter these measurements. For example, you can install switches at 36" above the floor in a child's bedroom, or set receptacles at 24" to make them more convenient for someone in a wheelchair.

Your inspector will check cables to see that they are anchored by cable staples driven within 8" of each box, and every 4 ft. thereafter when they run along studs. When bending cables, form the wire in a smooth curve. Do not crimp cables sharply or install them diagonally between framing members. Some inspectors specify that cables running between receptacle boxes should be about 20" above the floor.

What Inspectors Look For

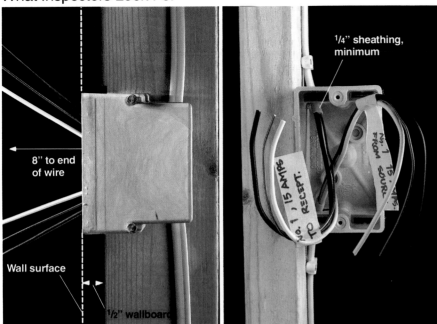

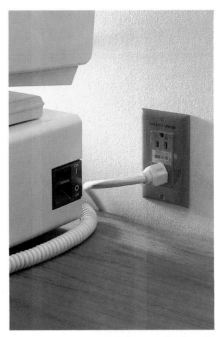

Electrical box faces should extend past the front of framing members so the boxes will be flush with finished walls (left). The inspector will check to see that all boxes are large enough for the wires they contain. Cables should be cut and stripped back so that 8" of usable length extends past the front of the box, and so that at least 1/4" of sheathing reaches into the box (right). Label all cables to show which circuits they serve: inspectors recognize this as a mark of careful work. The labels also simplify the final hookups after the wallboard is installed.

Install an isolated-ground circuit and receptacle if recommended by your inspector. An isolated-ground circuit protects sensitive electronic equipment, like a computer, against tiny current fluctuations. Computers also should be protected by a standard surge protector.

Heating & Air Conditioning Chart (compiled from manufacturers' literature)

Room Addition Living Area	Recommended Total Heating Rating	Recommended Circuit Size	Recommended Air-Conditioner Rating	Recommended Circuit Size
100 sq. feet	900 watts	15-amp (240 volts)	5,000 BTU	15-amp (120 volts)
150 sq. feet	1,350 watts		6,000 BTU	
200 sq. feet	1,800 watts		7,000 BTU	
300 sq. feet	2,700 watts		9,000 BTU	
400 sq. feet	3,600 watts	20-amp (240 volts)	10,500 BTU	
500 sq. feet	4,500 watts	30-amp (240 volts)	11,500 BTU	20-amp (120 volts)
800 sq. feet	7,200 watts	two 20-amp	17,000 BTU	15-amp (240 volts)
1,000 sq. feet	9,000 watts	two 30-amp	21,000 BTU	20-amp (240 volts)

Electric heating and air-conditioning for a new room addition will be checked by the inspector. Determine your heating and air-conditioning needs by finding the total area of the living space. Choose electric heating units with a combined wattage rating close to the chart recommendation above. Choose an air conditioner with a BTU rating close to the chart recommendation for your room size. NOTE: These recommendations are for homes in moderately cool climates, sometimes referred to as "Zone 4" regions. Cities in Zone 4 include Denver, Chicago, and Boston. In more severe climates, check with your electrical inspector or energy agency to learn how to find heating and air-conditioning needs.

4: Evaluate Electrical Loads

Before drawing a plan and applying for a work permit, make sure your home's electrical service provides enough power to handle the added load of the new circuits. In a safe wiring system, the current drawn by fixtures and appliances never exceeds the main service capacity.

To evaluate electrical loads, use the work sheet on page 17, or whatever evaluation method is recommended by your electrical inspector. Include the load for all existing wiring as well as that for the proposed new wiring when making your evaluation.

Most of the light fixtures and plug-in appliances in your home are evalutated as part of general allowances for basic lighting/receptacle circuits (page 9) and small-appliance circuits. However, appliances that are permanently installed require their own "dedicated" circuits. The electrical loads for these appliances are added in separately when evaluating wiring.

If your evaluation shows that the load exceeds the main service capacity, you must have an electrician upgrade the main service before you can install new wiring. An electrical service upgrade is a worthwhile investment that improves the value of your home and provides plenty of power for present and future wiring projects.

Tips for Evaluating Appliance Loads

Add 1500 watts for each small appliance circuit required by the local Electrical Code. In most communities, three such circuits are required—two in the kitchen and one for the laundry—for a total of 4500 watts. No further calculations are needed for appliances that plug into small-appliance or basic lighting/receptacle circuits.

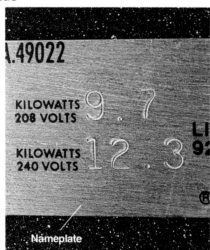

Nameplate

Find wattage ratings for permanent appliances by reading the manufacturer's nameplate. If the nameplate gives the rating in kilowatts, find the watts by multiplying kilowatts times 1000. If an appliance lists only amps, find watts by multiplying the amps times the voltage—either 120 or 240 volts.

Nameplate

Electric water heaters are permanent appliances that require their own dedicated 30-amp, 240-volt circuits. Most water heaters are rated between 3500 and 4500 watts. If the nameplate lists several wattage ratings, use the one labeled "total connected wattage" when figuring electrical loads.

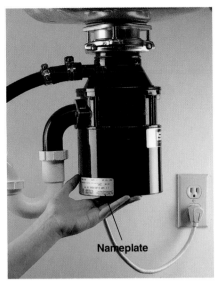

Food disposers are considered permanent appliances and require their own dedicated 15-amp, 120-volt circuits. Most disposers are rated between 500 and 900 watts.

Dishwashers installed permanently under a countertop need dedicated 15-amp, 120-volt circuits. Dishwasher ratings are usually between 1000 and 1500 watts. Portable dishwashers are regarded as part of small appliance circuits, and are not added in when figuring loads.

Electric ranges can be rated for as little as 3000 watts or as much as 12,000 watts. They require dedicated 120/240-volt circuits. Find the exact wattage rating by reading the nameplate, found inside the oven door or on the back of the unit.

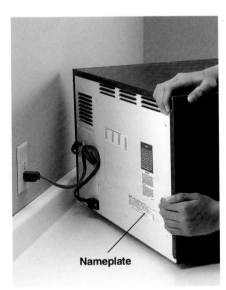

Microwave ovens are regarded by many local Codes as permanent appliances. If your inspector asks you to install a separate 20-amp, 120-volt circuit for the microwave oven, add in its wattage rating when calculating loads. The nameplate is found on the back of the cabinet or inside the front door. Most microwave ovens are rated between 500 and 800 watts.

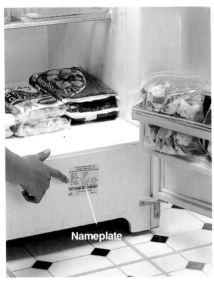

Freezers are permanent appliances that require dedicated 15-amp, 120-volt circuits. Freezer ratings are usually between 500 and 600 watts. But combination refrigerator-freezers rated for 1000 watts or less are plugged into small appliance circuits and do not need their own dedicated circuits. The nameplate for a freezer is found inside the door or on the back of the unit, just below the door seal.

Electric clothes dryers are permanent appliances that need dedicated 30-amp, 120/240-volt circuits. The wattage rating, usually between 4500 and 5500 watts, is printed on the nameplate inside the dryer door. Washing machines, and gas-heat clothes dryers with electric tumbler motors, do not need dedicated circuits. They plug into the 20-amp small-appliance circuit in the laundry.

(continued next page)

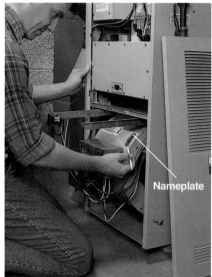

Forced-air furnaces have electric fans, and are considered permanent appliances. They require dedicated 15-amp, 120-volt circuits. Include the fan wattage rating, printed on a nameplate inside the control panel, when figuring wattage loads for heating.

A central air conditioner requires a dedicated 240-volt circuit. Its wattage rating, usually between 2300 and 5500 watts, is printed on a metal plate near the electrical hookup panel. If the air conditioner relies on a furnace fan for circulation, add the fan wattage rating to the air-conditioner rating.

Window air conditioners, both 120-volt and 240-volt types, are permanent appliances that require dedicated 15-amp or 20-amp circuits. The wattage rating, which can range from 500 to 2000 watts, is found on the nameplate located inside the front grill. Make sure to include all window air conditioners in your evaluation.

Electric room heaters that are permanently installed require a dedicated circuit, and must be figured into the load calculations. Use the maximum wattage rating printed inside the cover. As a general rule, 240-volt baseboard-type heaters are rated for about 250 watts for each linear foot.

Air-conditioning and heating appliances are not used at the same time, so figure in only the larger of these two numbers when evaluating your home's electrical load.

Outdoor receptacles and fixtures are not included in basic lighting calculations. When evaluating electrical loads, add in the nameplate wattage rating for each outdoor light fixture, and add in 180 watts for each outdoor receptacle. Receptacles and light fixtures in garages also are considered to be outdoor fixtures when evaluating loads.

How to Evaluate Electrical Loads (photocopy this work sheet as a guide; blue sample calculations will not reproduce)

1. Find the basic lighting/receptacle load by multiplying the square footage of all living areas (including any room additions) times 3 watts.	Existing space: _1100_ square ft. New additions: _400_ square ft. _1500_ total square ft. × 3 watts =	4500 watts
2. Add 1500 watts for each kitchen small-appliance circuit and for the laundry circuit.	_3_ circuits × 1500 watts =	4500 watts
3. Add ratings for permanent electrical appliances, including: range, food disposer, dishwasher, freezer, water heater, and clothes dryer.	RANGE 12.3 K.W. = 12,300 WATTS	12,300 watts
	DRYER 5000	5,000 watts
	DISHWASHER 1200	1,200 watts
	FREEZER 550	550 watts
	FOOD DISPOSER 800	800 watts
Find total wattages for the furnace and heating units, and for air conditioners. Add in only the larger of these numbers.	Furnace heat: _1200_ watts Space heaters: _5450_ watts Total heating = _6650_ watts	6,650 watts
	Central air conditioner: _3500_ watts Window air conditioners: _1100_ watts Total cooling = _4600_ watts	
4. For outdoor fixtures (including those in garages) find the nameplate wattage ratings.	Total fixture watts =	650 watts
Multiply the number of outdoor receptacles (including those in garages) times 180 watts.	_3_ receptacles × 180 watts =	540 watts
5. Total the wattages to find the gross load.		36,690 watts
6. Figure the first 10,000 watts of the gross load at 100%.	100% × 10,000 = 10,000	10,000 watts
7. Subtract 10,000 watts from the gross load, then figure the remaining load at 40%.	_36,690_ watts - 10,000 = _26,690_ watts _26,690_ watts × .40 =	10,676 watts
8. Add steps 6 and 7 to estimate the true electrical load.		20,676 watts
9. Convert the estimated true electrical load to amps by dividing by 230.	_20,676_ watts ÷ 230 =	89.9 amps
10. Compare the load with the amp rating of your home's electrical service, printed on the main circuit breaker (page 8). If the load is less than main circuit breaker rating, the system is safe. If the load exceeds the main circuit breaker rating, your service should be upgraded.		OK ☑ Upgrade ☐

A detailed wiring diagram and a list of materials is required before your electrical inspector will issue a work permit. If blueprints exist for the space you are remodeling, start your electrical diagram by tracing the wall outlines from the blueprint. Use standard electrical symbols (page opposite) to clearly show all the receptacles, switches, light fixtures, and permanent appliances. Make a copy of the symbol key, and attach it to the wiring diagram for the inspector's convenience. Show each cable run, and label its wire size and circuit amperage.

Planning a Wiring Project

5: Draw a Wiring Diagram & Get a Permit

Drawing a wiring diagram is the last step in planning a circuit installation. A detailed wiring diagram helps you get a work permit, makes it easy to create a list of materials, and serves as a guide for laying out circuits and installing cables and fixtures. Use the circuit maps on pages 20 to 31 as a guide for planning wiring configurations and cable runs. Bring the diagram and materials list when you visit the electrical inspector to apply for a work permit.

Never install new wiring without following your community's permit and inspection procedure. A work permit is not expensive, and it ensures that your work will be reviewed by a qualified inspector to guarantee its safety. If you install new wiring without the proper permit, an accident or fire traced to faulty wiring could cause your insurance company to discontinue your policy, and can hurt the resale value of your home.

When the electrical inspector looks over your wiring diagram, he will ask questions to see if you have a basic understanding of the Electrical Code and fundamental wiring skills. Some inspectors ask these questions informally, while others give a short written test. The inspector may allow you to do some, but not all, of the work. For example, he may ask that all final circuit connections at the circuit breaker panel be made by a licensed electrician, while allowing you to do all other work.

A few communities allow you to install wiring only when supervised by an electrician. This means you can still install your own wiring, but must hire an electrician to apply for the work permit and to check your work before the inspector reviews it. The electrician is held responsible for the quality of the job.

Remember that it is your inspector's responsibility to help you do a safe and professional job. Feel free to call him with questions about wiring techniques or materials.

How to Draw a Wiring Plan

1 Draw a scaled diagram of the space you will be wiring, showing walls, doors, windows, plumbing pipes and fixtures, and heating and cooling ducts. Find the floor space by multiplying room length by width, and indicate this on the diagram. Do not include closets or storage areas when figuring space.

2 Mark the location of all switches, receptacles, light fixtures, and permanent appliances, using the electrical symbols shown below. Where you locate these devices along the cable run determines how they are wired. Use the circuit maps on pages 20 to 31 as a guide for drawing wiring diagrams.

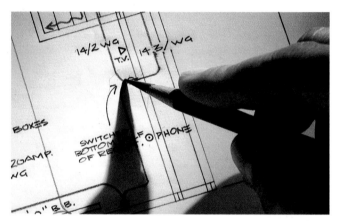

3 Draw in cable runs between devices. Indicate cable size and type, and the amperage of the circuits. Use a different-colored pencil for each circuit.

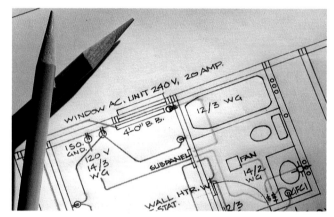

4 Identify the wattages for light fixtures and permanent appliances, and the type and size of each electrical box. On another sheet of paper, make a detailed list of all materials you will use.

Electrical Symbol Key (copy this key and attach it to your wiring plan)

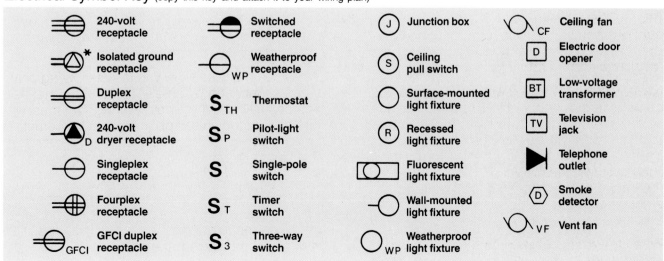

240-volt receptacle	Switched receptacle	Junction box
Isolated ground receptacle	Weatherproof receptacle	Ceiling pull switch
Duplex receptacle	S TH Thermostat	Surface-mounted light fixture
240-volt dryer receptacle	S P Pilot-light switch	Recessed light fixture
Singleplex receptacle	S Single-pole switch	Fluorescent light fixture
Fourplex receptacle	S T Timer switch	Wall-mounted light fixture
GFCI duplex receptacle	S 3 Three-way switch	Weatherproof light fixture
		CF Ceiling fan
		D Electric door opener
		BT Low-voltage transformer
		TV Television jack
		Telephone outlet
		D Smoke detector
		VF Vent fan

Glossary of Electrical Terms

Ampacity: A measurement of how many amps can be safely carried by a wire or cable. Ampacity varies according to the diameter of the wire (page 43).

Common wire: The hot circuit wire that brings current from the power source to a three-way switch, or that carries current from a three-way switch to a light fixture. A common wire is always connected to the darker screw terminal on the switch, sometimes labeled COMMON.

Dedicated circuit: An electrical circuit that serves only one appliance or series of electric heaters.

EMT: *Electrical Metallic Tubing.* A type of metal conduit used for exposed indoor wiring installations, such as wiring in an unfinished basement.

Feeder cable: The length of cable that carries power from the main circuit breaker panel to the first electrical box in a circuit, or from the main panel to a circuit breaker subpanel. Also known as a *home run.*

GFCI: A duplex receptacle or circuit breaker rated as a *Ground-Fault Circuit-Interrupter.* GFCI receptacles provide extra protection against shock and are required by Code in some locations.

Home run: See *Feeder cable*

IMC: *Intermediate Metallic Conduit.* Sturdier than EMT, IMC conduit is used for exposed wiring both indoors and outdoors.

Isolated-ground circuit: A 120-volt circuit installed with three-wire cable that protects sensitive electronic equipment, like a computer, against power surges.

Isolated-ground receptacle: A special-use receptacle, orange in color, with an insulated grounding screw. Used to protect computers or other sensitive electronic equipment against power surges.

Line side wires: Circuit wires that extend "upstream" from an electrical box, toward the power source.

Load side wires: Circuit wires extending "downstream" from an electrical box toward end of circuit.

NM cable: *Non-Metallic sheathed cable.* The standard cable used for indoor wiring inside finished walls.

Pigtail: A short length of wire used to join two or more circuit wires to the same screw terminal on a receptacle, switch, or metal electrical box. Pigtails are color-coded to match the wires they are connected to.

PVC: *Poly-Vinyl Chloride.* A durable plastic used for electrical boxes and conduit. Can be used instead of metal conduit to protect outdoor wiring.

Shared Neutral: When two 120-volt small-appliance circuits are wired using a single three-wire cable, the white circuit wire is a *shared neutral* that serves both circuits.

Split receptacle: A duplex receptacle in which the connecting tab linking the brass screw terminals has been broken. A split receptacle is required when one half of a duplex receptacle is controlled by a switch, or when each half is controlled by a different circuit.

THHN/THWN wires: The type of wire that is recommended for installation inside metal or plastic conduit. Available as individual conductors with color-coded insulation.

Three-wire cable: Sheathed cable with one black, one white, and one red insulated conductor, plus a bare copper grounding wire.

Traveler wires: In a three-way switch configuration, two *traveler wires* run between the pairs of traveler screw terminals on the three-way switches.

Two-wire cable: Sheathed cable with one black and one white insulated conductor plus a bare copper grounding wire.

UF Cable: *Underground Feeder* cable. Used for outdoor wiring, UF cable is rated for direct contact with soil.

Circuit Maps for 24 Common Wiring Layouts

The arrangement of switches and appliances along an electrical circuit differs for every project. This means that the configuration of wires inside an electrical box can vary greatly, even when fixtures are identical.

The circuit maps on the following pages show the most common wiring variations for typical electrical devices. Most new wiring you install will match one or more of the examples shown. By finding the examples that match your situation, you can use these maps to plan circuit layouts.

The 120-volt circuits shown on the following pages are wired for 15 amps, using 14-gauge wire and receptacles rated at 15 amps. If you

are installing a 20-amp circuit, substitute 12-gauge cables and use receptacles rated for 20 amps.

In configurations where a white wire serves as a hot wire instead of a neutral, both ends of the wire are coded with black tape to identify it as hot. In addition, each of the circuit maps shows a box grounding screw. This grounding screw is required in all metal boxes, but plastic electrical boxes do not need to be grounded.

NOTE: For clarity, all grounding conductors in the circuit maps are colored green. In practice, the grounding wires inside sheathed cables usually are bare copper.

1. 120-volt Duplex Receptacles Wired in Sequence

Use this layout to link any number of duplex receptacles ~~in~~ basic lighting/receptacle circuit. The last receptacle ~~in~~ the cable run is connected like the receptacle ~~shown~~ at the right side of the circuit map below. ~~Other~~ receptacles are wired like the receptacle shown on the left side. Requires two-wire cables.

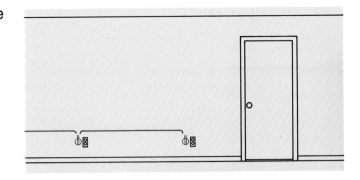

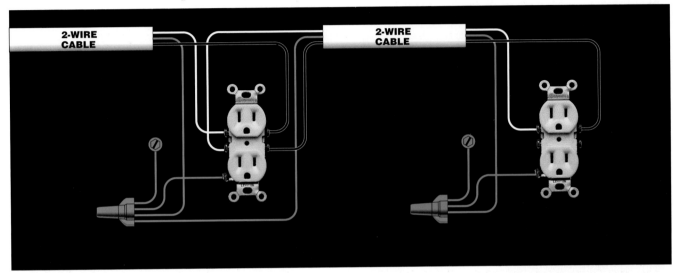

2. GFCI Receptacles (Single-location Protection)

Use this layout when receptacles are within 6 ft. of a water source, like those in kitchens and bathrooms. To prevent "nuisance tripping" caused by normal power surges, GFCIs should be connected only at the LINE screw terminal, so they protect a single location, not the fixtures on the LOAD side of the circuit. Requires two-wire cables. Where a GFCI must protect other fixtures, use circuit map 3.

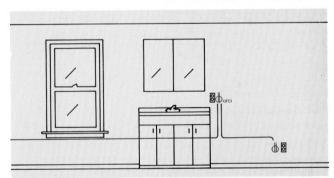

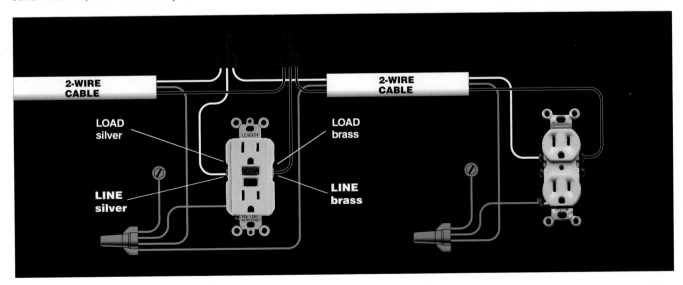

3. GFCI Receptacle, Switch & Light Fixture (Wired for Multiple-location Protection)

In some locations, such as an outdoor circuit, it is a good idea to connect a GFCI receptacle so it also provides shock protection to the wires and fixtures that continue to the end of the circuit. Wires from the power source are connected to the LINE screw terminals; outgoing wires are connected to LOAD screws. Requires two-wire cables.

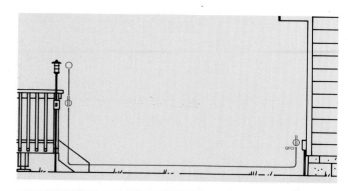

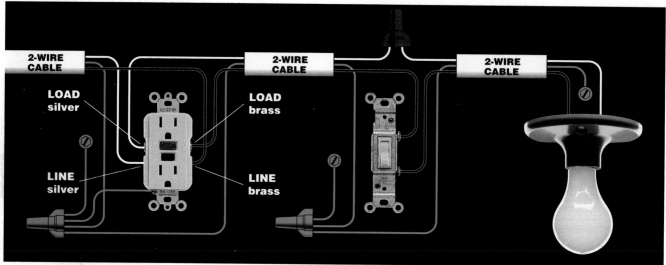

4. Single-pole Switch & Light Fixture (Light Fixture at End of Cable Run)

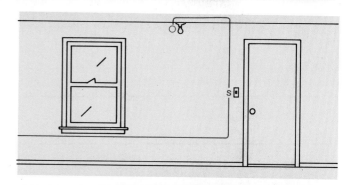

Use this layout for light fixtures in basic lighting/receptacle circuits throughout the home. It is often used as an extension to a series of receptacles (circuit map 1). Requires two-wire cables.

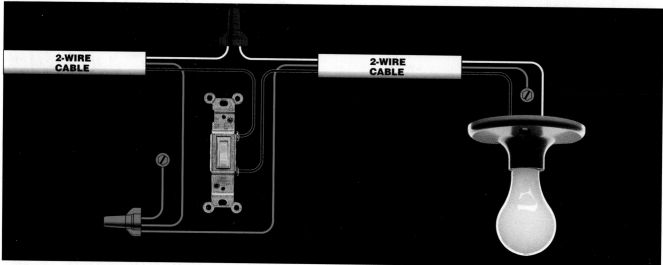

5. Single-pole Switch & Light Fixture (Switch at End of Cable Run)

Use this layout, sometimes called a "switch loop," where it is more practical to locate a switch at the end of the cable run. In the last length of cable, both insulated wires are hot; the white wire is tagged with black tape at both ends to indicate it is hot. Requires two-wire cables.

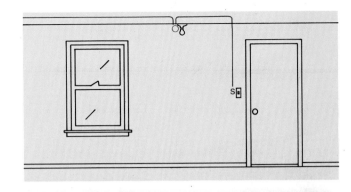

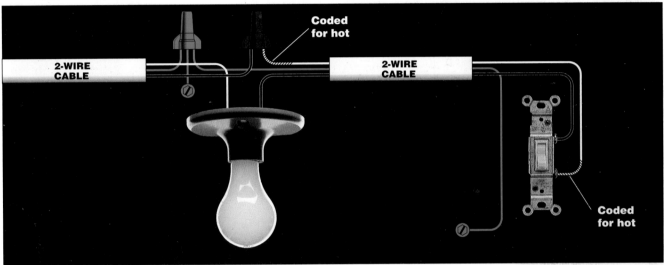

6. Single-pole Switch & Light Fixture, Duplex Receptacle (Switch at Start of Cable Run)

Use this layout to continue a circuit past a switched light fixture to one or more duplex receptacles. To add multiple receptacles to the circuit, see circuit map 1. Requires two-wire and three-wire cables.

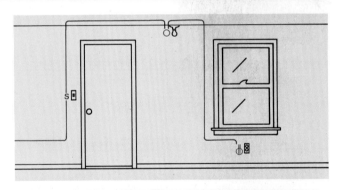

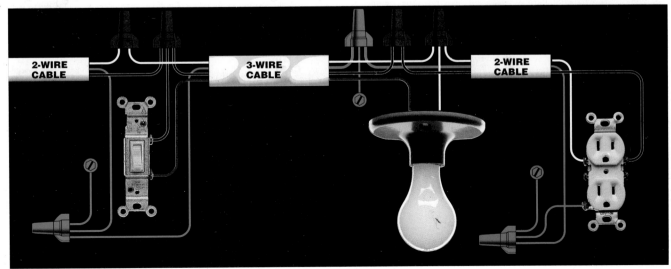

7. Switch-controlled Split Receptacle, Duplex Receptacle (Switch at Start of Cable Run)

This layout lets you use a wall switch to control a lamp plugged into a wall receptacle. This configuration is required by Code for any room that does not have a switch-controlled ceiling fixture. Only the bottom half of the first receptacle is controlled by the wall switch; the top half of the receptacle and all additional receptacles on the circuit are always hot. Requires two-wire and three-wire cables.

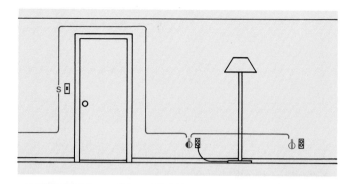

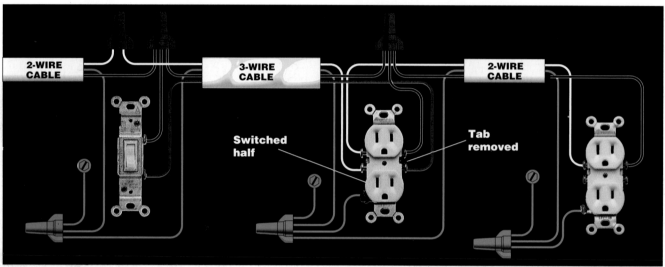

8. Switch-controlled Split Receptacle (Switch at End of Cable Run)

Use this "switch loop" layout to control a split receptacle (see circuit map 7) from an end-of-run circuit location. The bottom half of the receptacle is controlled by the wall switch, while the top half is always hot. White circuit wire attached to the switch is tagged with black tape to indicate it is hot. Requires two-wire cable.

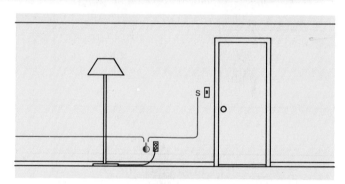

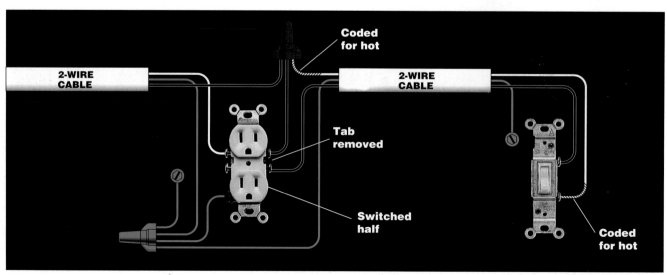

9. Switch-controlled Split Receptacle, Duplex Receptacle (Split Receptacle at Start of Run)

Use this variation of circuit map 7 where it is more practical to locate a switch-controlled receptacle at the start of a cable run. Only the bottom half of the first receptacle is controlled by the wall switch; the top half of the receptacle, and all other receptacles on the circuit, are always hot. Requires two-wire and three-wire cables.

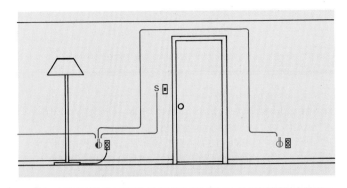

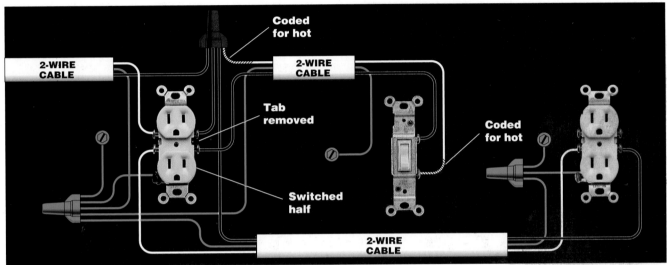

10. Double Receptacle Circuit with Shared Neutral Wire (Receptacles Alternate Circuits)

This layout features two 120-volt circuits wired with one three-wire cable connected to a double-pole circuit breaker. The black hot wire powers one circuit, the red wire powers the other. The white wire is a shared neutral that serves both circuits. When wired with 12/2 and 12/3 cable, and receptacles rated for 20 amps, this layout can be used for the two small-appliance circuits required in a kitchen.

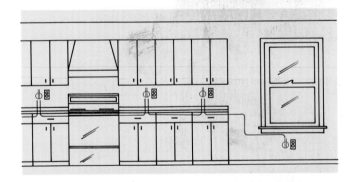

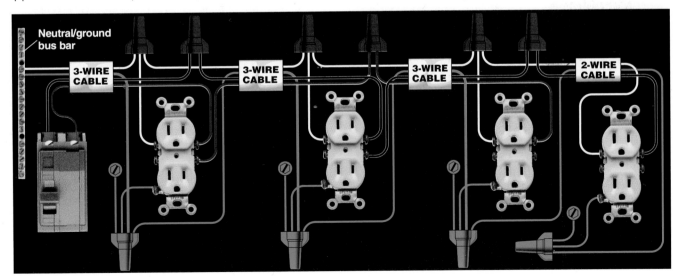

11. Double Receptacle Circuit with GFCIs & Shared Neutral Wire

Use this layout variation of circuit map 10 to wire a double receptacle circuit when Code requires that some of the receptacles be GFCIs. The GFCIs should be wired for single-location protection (see circuit map 2). Requires three-wire and two-wire cables.

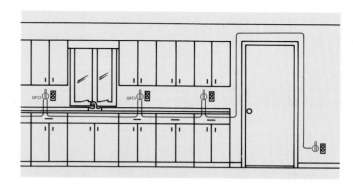

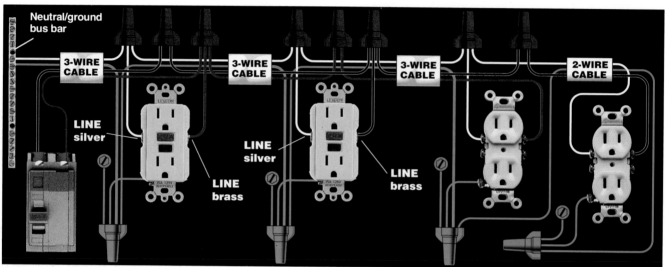

12. 240-volt Appliance Receptacle

This layout represents a 20-amp, 240-volt dedicated appliance circuit wired with 12/2 cable, as required by Code for a large window air conditioner. Receptacles are available in both singleplex (shown) and duplex styles. The black and white circuit wires connected to a double-pole breaker each bring 120 volts of power to the receptacle. The white wire is tagged with black tape to indicate it is hot.

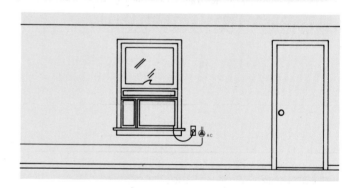

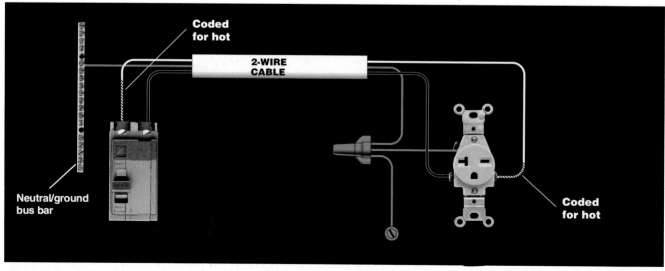

13. 240-volt Baseboard Heaters, Thermostat

This layout is typical for a series of 240-volt baseboard heaters controlled by wall thermostat. Except for the last heater in the circuit, all heaters are wired as shown below. The last heater is connected to only one cable. The size of the circuit and cables are determined by finding the total wattage of all heaters (page 13). Requires two-wire cable.

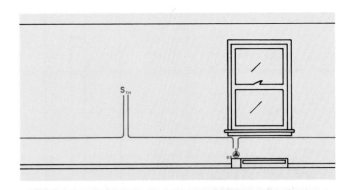

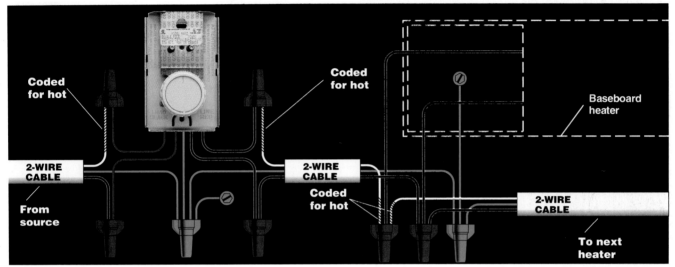

14. 120/240-volt Appliance Receptacle

This layout is for a 50-amp, 120/240-volt dedicated appliance circuit wired with 6/3 cable, as required by Code for a large kitchen range. The black and red circuit wires, connected to a double-pole circuit breaker in the circuit breaker panel, each bring 120 volts of power to the setscrew terminals on the receptacle. The white circuit wire attached to the neutral bus bar in the circuit breaker panel is connected to the neutral setscrew terminal on the receptacle.

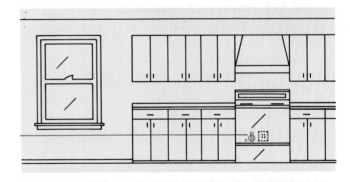

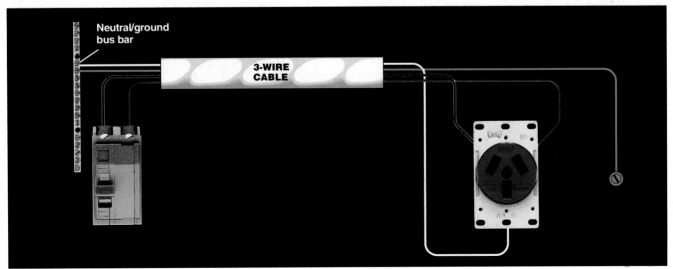

15. Dedicated 120-volt Computer Circuit, Isolated-ground Receptacle

This 15-amp circuit provides extra protection against power surges that can harm computers. It uses 14/3 cable in which the red wire serves as an extra grounding conductor. The red wire is tagged with green tape for identification. It is connected to the grounding screw on an "isolated-ground" receptacle, and runs back to the grounding bus bar in the circuit breaker panel without touching any other house wiring.

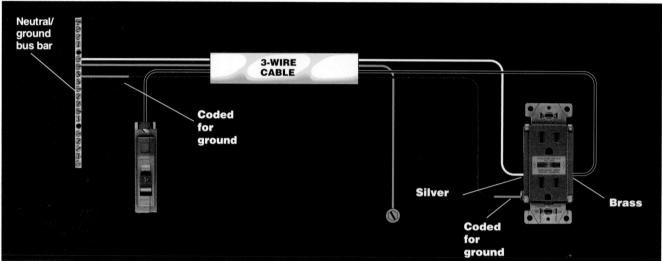

16. Ganged Single-pole Switches Controlling Separate Light Fixtures

This layout lets you place two switches controlled by the same 120-volt circuit in one double-gang electrical box. A single feed cable provides power to both switches. A similar layout with two feed cables can be used to place switches from different circuits in the same box. Requires two-wire cable.

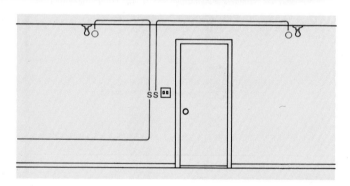

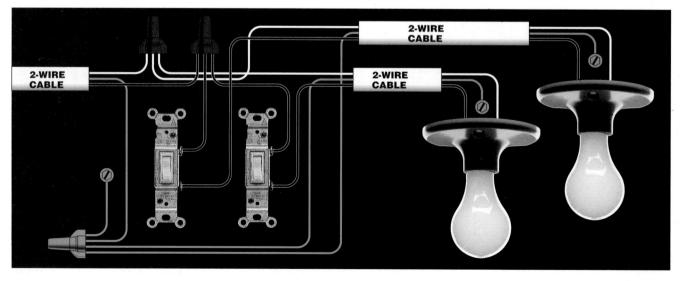

17. Three-way Switches & Light Fixture (Fixture Between Switches)

This layout for three-way switches lets you control a light fixture from two locations. Each switch has one COMMON screw terminal and two TRAVELER screws. Circuit wires attached to the TRAVELER screws run between the two switches, and hot wires attached to the COMMON screws bring current from the power source and carry it to the light fixture. Requires two-wire and three-wire cables.

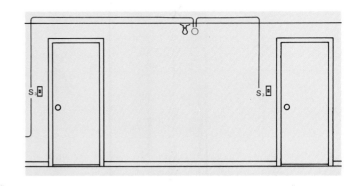

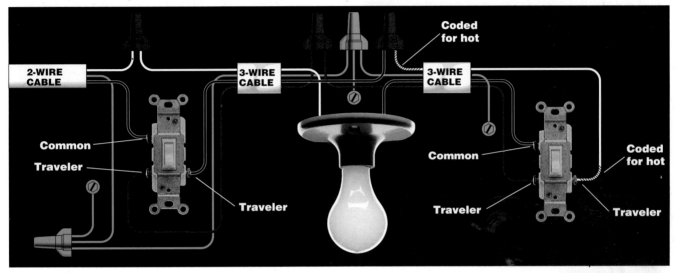

18. Three-way Switches & Light Fixture (Fixture at Start of Cable Run)

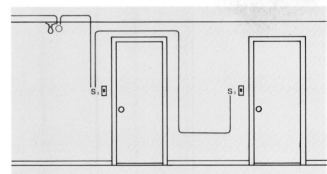

Use this layout variation of circuit map 17 where it is more convenient to locate the fixture ahead of the three-way switches in the cable run. Requires two-wire and three-wire cables.

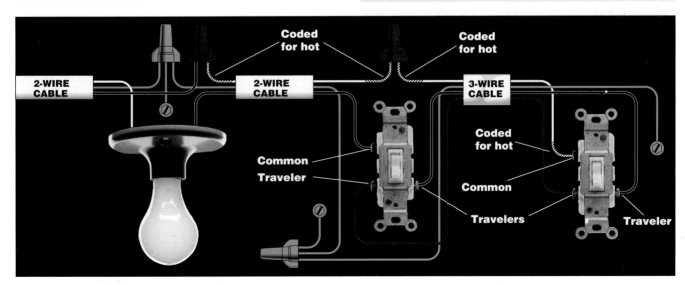

29

19. Three-way Switches & Light Fixture (Fixture at End of Cable Run)

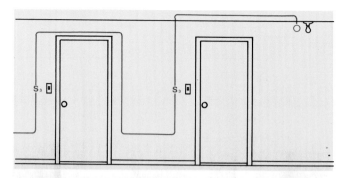

This alternate variation of the three-way switch layout (circuit map 17) is used where it is more practical to locate the fixture at the end of the cable run. Requires two-wire and three-wire cables.

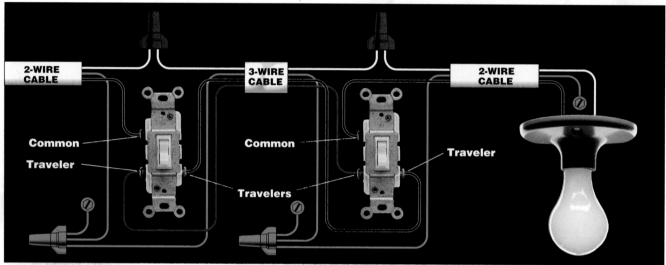

20. Three-way Switches & Light Fixture with Duplex Receptacle

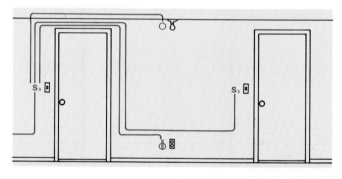

Use this layout to add a receptacle to a three-way switch configuration (circuit map 17). Requires two-wire and three-wire cables.

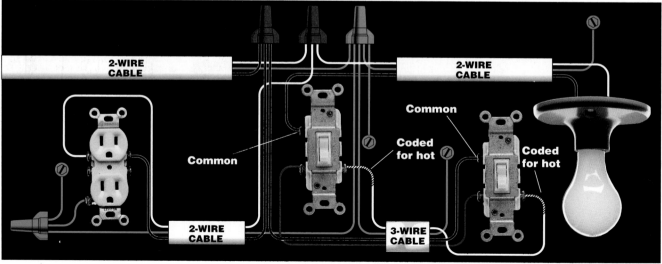

21. Ceiling Fan/Light Fixture Controlled by Ganged Switches (Fan at End of Cable Run)

This layout is for a combination ceiling fan/light fixture, controlled by a speed-control switch and dimmer in a double-gang switch box. Requires two-wire and three-wire cables.

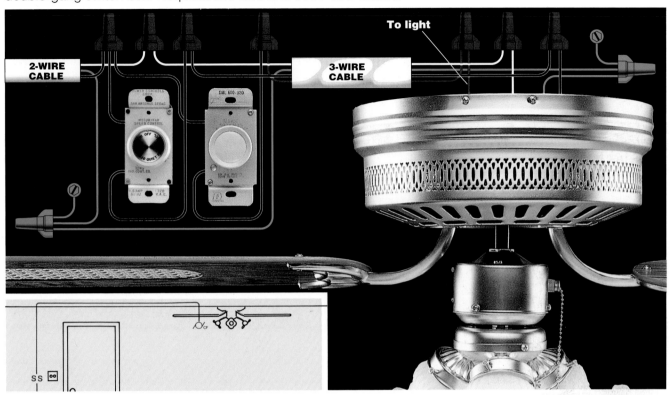

22. Ceiling Fan/Light Fixture Controlled by Ganged Switches (Switches at End of Cable Run)

Use this "switch loop" layout variation when it is more practical to install the ganged speed control and dimmer switches for the ceiling fan at the end of the cable run. Requires two-wire and three-wire cables.

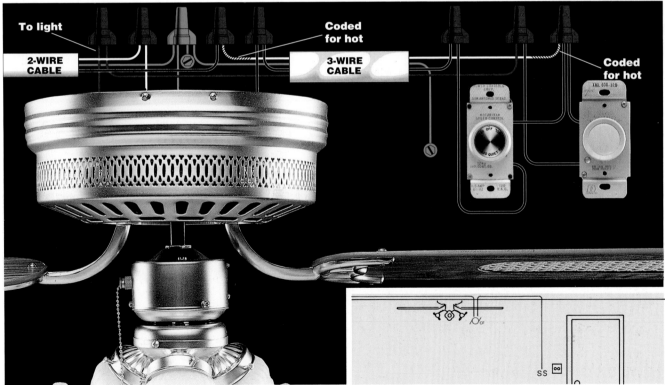

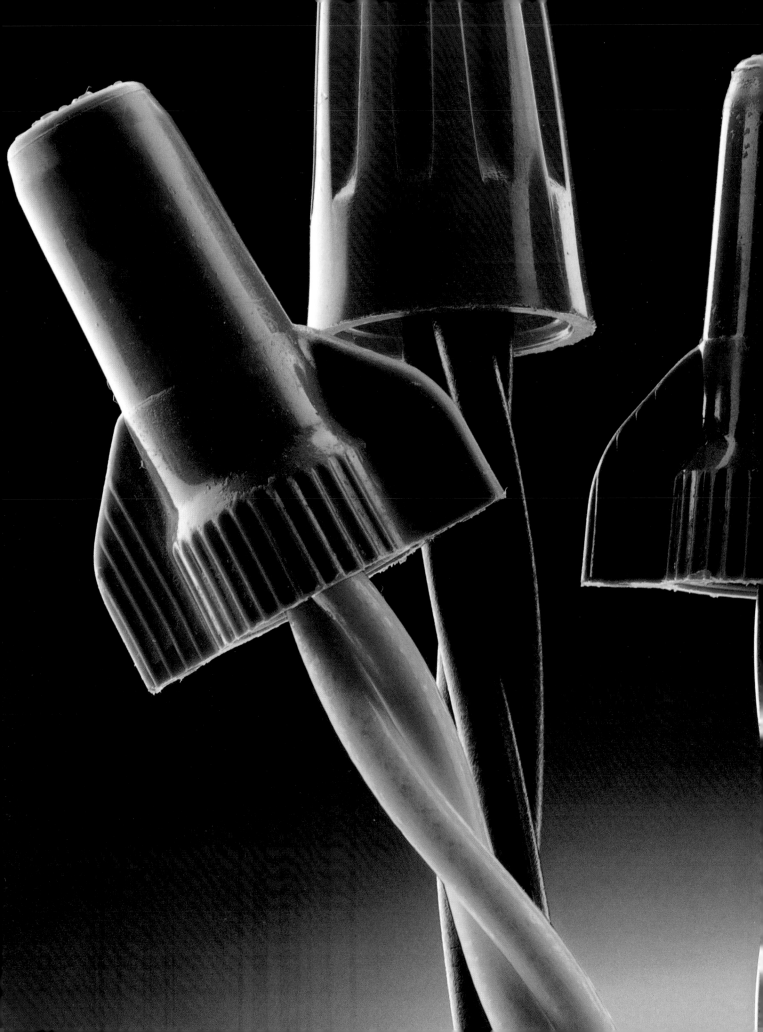

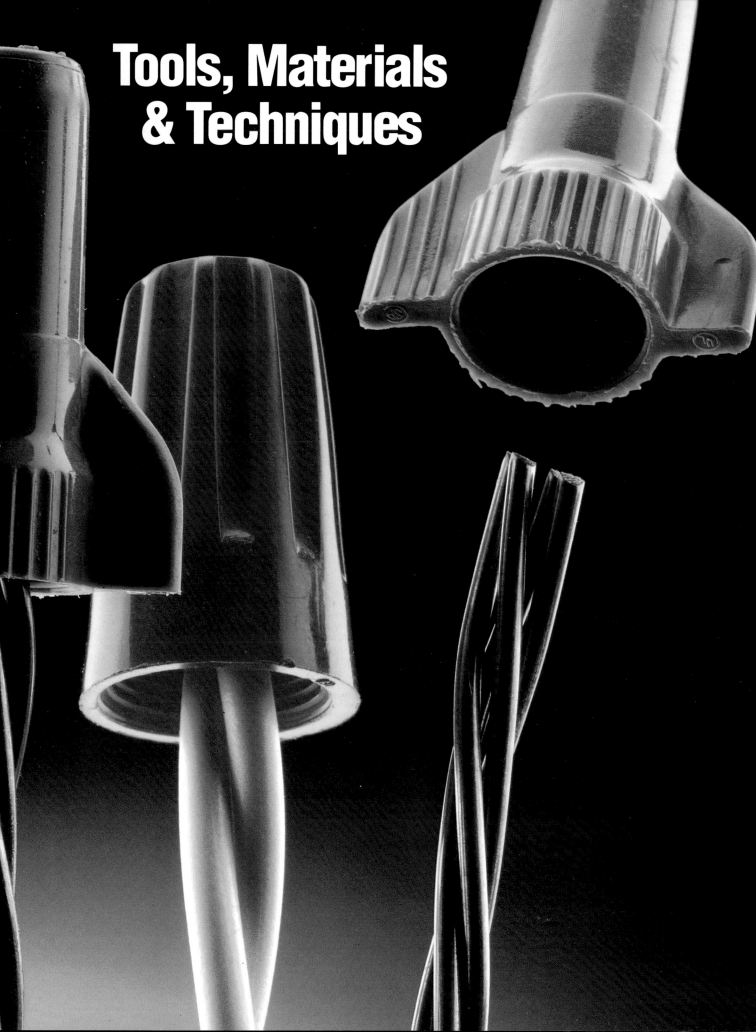

Tools, Materials
& Techniques

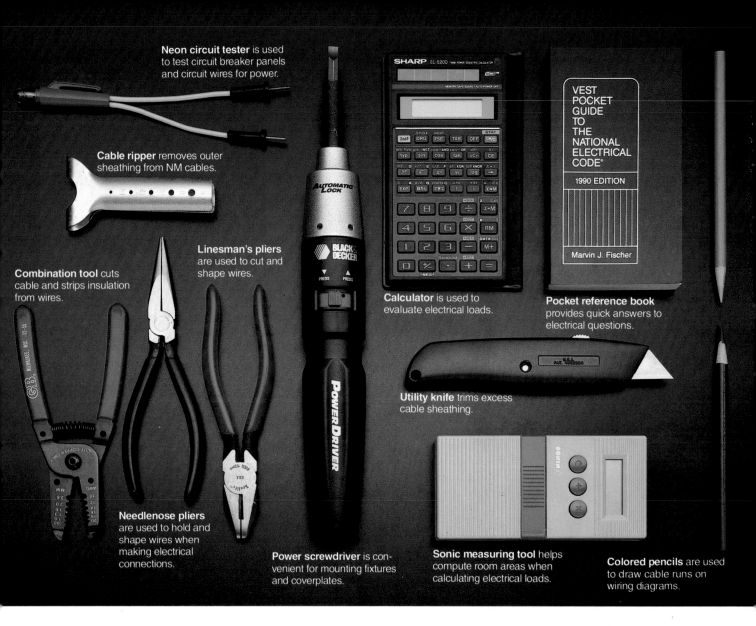

Neon circuit tester is used to test circuit breaker panels and circuit wires for power.

Cable ripper removes outer sheathing from NM cables.

Linesman's pliers are used to cut and shape wires.

Combination tool cuts cable and strips insulation from wires.

Calculator is used to evaluate electrical loads.

VEST POCKET GUIDE TO THE NATIONAL ELECTRICAL CODE®

1990 EDITION

Marvin J. Fischer

Pocket reference book provides quick answers to electrical questions.

Utility knife trims excess cable sheathing.

Needlenose pliers are used to hold and shape wires when making electrical connections.

Power screwdriver is convenient for mounting fixtures and coverplates.

Sonic measuring tool helps compute room areas when calculating electrical loads.

Colored pencils are used to draw cable runs on wiring diagrams.

Tools, Materials & Techniques

To complete the wiring projects shown in this book, you need a few specialty electrical tools (above), as well as a basic collection of hand tools (page opposite). As with any tool purchase, invest in good-quality products when you buy tools for electrical work. Keep your tools clean, and sharpen or replace any cutting tools that have dull edges.

The materials used for electrical wiring have changed dramatically in the last 20 years, making it much easier for homeowners to do their own electrical work. The following pages show how to work with the following components:

- Electrical boxes (pages 36 to 41).
- Wires & cables (pages 42 to 49).
- Conduit (pages 50 to 55).
- Circuit breaker panels (pages 56 to 57).
- Circuit breakers (pages 58 to 59).
- Subpanels (pages 56 to 57, 60 to 63).

Plastic electrical boxes for indoor installations are ideal for do-it-yourself electrical work. They have preattached mounting nails for easy installation and are much less expensive than metal boxes.

Screwdrivers with insulated handles are used to assemble fixtures and make wire connections.

Tool belt keeps a wide variety of tools within easy reach.

Tape measure is used to position electrical boxes and determine cable lengths.

Nut driver and adjustable wrench are used to assemble and mount electrical fixtures.

Electrical tapes are used for marking wires and for attaching cables to a fish tape.

A fish tape is useful for installing cables in finished wall cavities and for pulling wires through conduit. Products designed for lubrication reduce friction and make it easier to pull cables and wires.

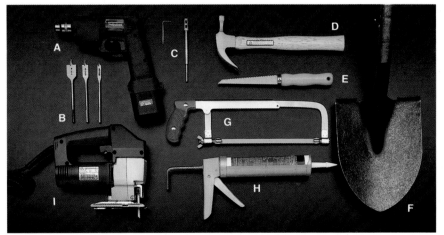

These basic tools are used for advanced wiring projects: drill (A), spade bits (B), and drill bit extension (C) for boring holes in framing members; hammer (D) for attaching electrical boxes; wallboard saw (E) for making cutouts in indoor walls; shovel (F) to dig trenches for outdoor wiring; hacksaw (G) for cutting conduit; caulk gun (H) for sealing gaps in exterior walls; jig saw (I) for making wall cutouts.

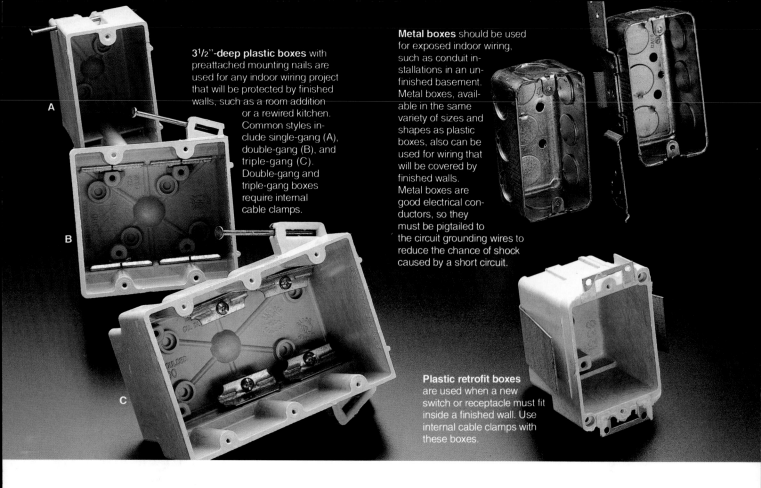

3¹/₂"-deep plastic boxes with preattached mounting nails are used for any indoor wiring project that will be protected by finished walls, such as a room addition or a rewired kitchen. Common styles include single-gang (A), double-gang (B), and triple-gang (C). Double-gang and triple-gang boxes require internal cable clamps.

Metal boxes should be used for exposed indoor wiring, such as conduit installations in an unfinished basement. Metal boxes, available in the same variety of sizes and shapes as plastic boxes, also can be used for wiring that will be covered by finished walls. Metal boxes are good electrical conductors, so they must be pigtailed to the circuit grounding wires to reduce the chance of shock caused by a short circuit.

Plastic retrofit boxes are used when a new switch or receptacle must fit inside a finished wall. Use internal cable clamps with these boxes.

Electrical Boxes

Use the chart below to select the proper type of box for your wiring project. For most indoor wiring done with NM cable, use plastic electrical boxes. Plastic boxes are inexpensive, lightweight, and easy to install.

Metal boxes also can be used for indoor NM cable installations and are still favored by some electricians, especially for supporting heavy ceiling light fixtures.

If you have choice of box depths, always choose the deepest size available. Wire connections are easier to make if boxes are roomy. Check with your local inspector if you have questions regarding the proper box size to use.

Box type	Typical Uses
Plastic	• Protected indoor wiring, used with NM cable • Not suited for heavy light fixtures and fans
Metal	• Exposed indoor wiring, used with metal conduit • Protected indoor wiring, used with NM cable
Cast aluminum	• Outdoor wiring, used with metal conduit
PVC plastic	• Outdoor wiring, used with PVC conduit • Exposed indoor wiring, used with PVC conduit

Tips for Using Electrical Boxes

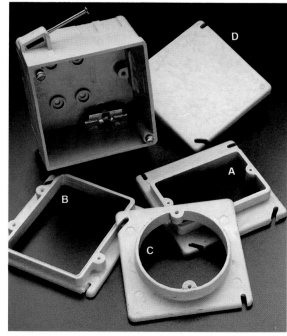

A square plastic box, 4" × 4" × 3" deep, provides extra space for making wire connections. It has preattached nails for easy mounting. A variety of adapter plates are available for 4" × 4" boxes, including single-gang (A), double-gang (B), light fixture (C), and junction box coverplate (D). Adapter plates come in several thicknesses to match different wall constructions.

Plastic retrofit light fixture box lets you install a new fixture in an existing wall or ceiling.

Plastic light fixture boxes with brace bars let you position a fixture between framing members.

Metal light fixture boxes with heavy-duty brace bars are recommended when installing heavy light fixtures or hanging a ceiling fan.

Cast aluminum boxes are required for outdoor electrical fixtures connected with metal conduit. Cast aluminum boxes have sealed seams and threaded openings to keep moisture out. A variety of weatherproof coverplates are available, including duplex receptacle plates (A), GFCI receptacle plates (B), and switch plates.

PVC plastic boxes are used with PVC conduit in outdoor wiring and exposed indoor wiring. Many local codes now allow the use of PVC plastic boxes. PVC coverplates are available to fit switches, standard duplex receptacles, and GFCI receptacles.

Boxes larger than 2" × 4", and all retrofit boxes, must have internal cable clamps. After installing cables in the box, tighten the cable clamps over the cables so they are gripped firmly, but not so tightly that the cable sheathing is crushed.

Metal boxes must be grounded to the circuit grounding system. Connect the circuit grounding wires to the box with a green insulated pigtail wire and wire nut (as shown) or with a grounding clip (page 50).

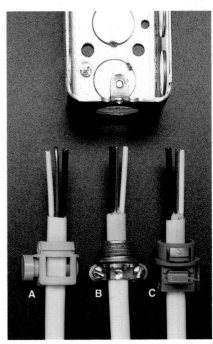

Cables entering a metal box must be clamped. A variety of clamps are available, including plastic clamps (A, C) and threaded metal clamps (B).

Installing Electrical Boxes

Install electrical boxes for receptacles, switches, and fixtures only after your wiring project plan has been approved by your inspector. Use your wiring plan as a guide, and follow electrical Code height and spacing guidelines when laying out box positions.

Always use the deepest electrical boxes that are practical for your installation. Using deep boxes ensures that you will meet Code regulations regarding box volume, and makes it easier to make the wire connections.

Some electrical fixtures, like recessed light fixtures, electric heaters, and exhaust fans, have built-in wire connection boxes. Install the frames for these fixtures at the same time you are installing the other electrical boxes.

Electrical boxes in adjacent rooms should be positioned close together when they share a common wall and are controlled by the same circuit. This simplifies the cable installations and also reduces the amount of cable needed.

Fixtures That Do Not Need Electrical Boxes

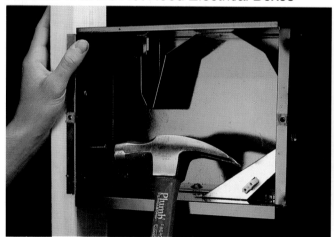

Wire connection box

Recessed fixtures that fit inside wall cavities have built-in wire connection boxes, and require no additional electrical boxes. Common recessed fixtures include electric blower-heaters (above, left), bathroom vent fans (above, right), and recessed light fixtures (page 98). Install the frames for these fixtures at the same time you are installing the other electrical boxes along the circuit. **Surface-mounted fixtures,** like electric baseboard heaters (page 87) and under-cabinet fluorescent lights (page 105), also have built-in wire connection boxes. These fixtures are not installed until it is time to make the final hookups.

How to Install Electrical Boxes for Receptacles

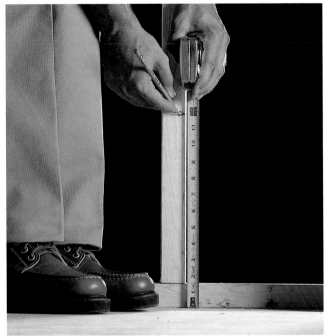

1 Mark the location of each box on studs. Standard receptacle boxes should be centered 12" above floor level. GFCI receptacle boxes in a bathroom should be mounted so they will be about 10" above the finished countertop.

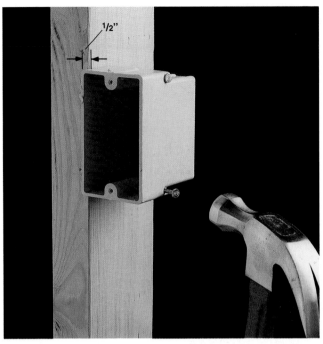

2 Position each box against a stud so the front face will be flush with the finished wall. For example, if you will be installing 1/2" wallboard, position the box so it extends 1/2" past the face of the stud. Anchor the box by driving the mounting nails into the stud.

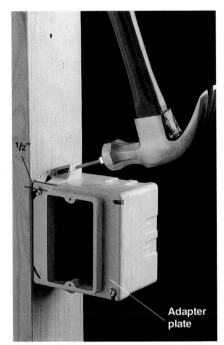

3 If installing 4" × 4" boxes, attach the adapter plates before positioning the boxes. Use adapter plates that match the thickness of the finished wall. Anchor the box by driving the mounting nails into the stud.

Adapter plate

4 Open one knockout for each cable that will enter the box, using a hammer and screwdriver.

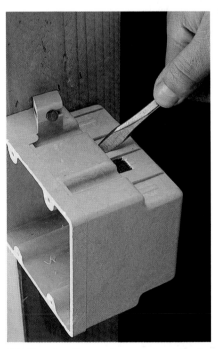

5 Break off any sharp edges that might damage vinyl cable sheathing by rotating a screwdriver in the knockout.

How to Install Boxes for Light Fixtures

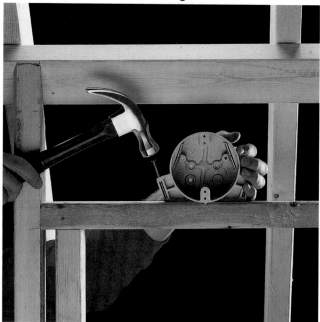

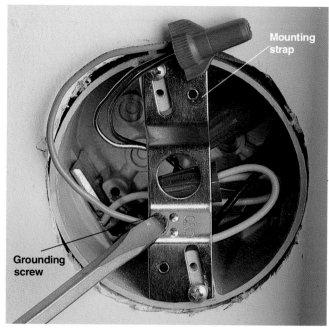

Position a light fixture box for a vanity light above the frame opening for a mirror or medicine cabinet. Place the box for a ceiling light fixture in the center of the room. The box for a stairway light should be mounted so every step will be lighted. Position each box against a framing member so the front face will be flush with the finished wall or ceiling, then anchor the box by driving the mounting nails into the framing member.

Attach a mounting strap to the box if one is required by the light-fixture manufacturer. Mounting straps are needed where the fixture mounting screws do not match the holes in the electrical box. A pre-attached grounding screw on the strap provides a place to pigtail grounding wires.

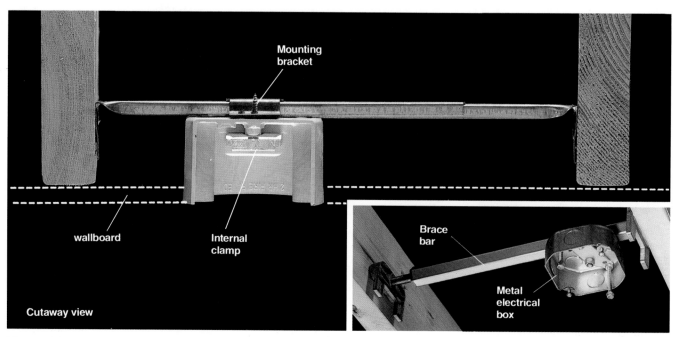

To position a light fixture between joists, attach an electrical box to an adjustable brace bar. Nail the ends of the brace bar to joists so the face of the box will be flush with the finished ceiling surface. Slide the box along the brace bar to the desired position,

then tighten the mounting screws. Use internal cable clamps when using a box with a brace bar. NOTE: For ceiling fans and heavy light fixtures, use a metal box and a heavy-duty brace bar rated for heavy loads (inset photo).

How to Install Boxes for Switches

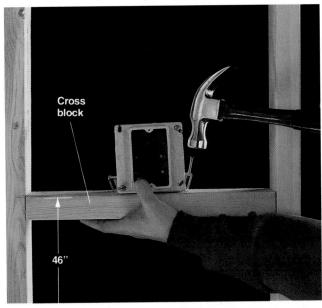

Install switch boxes at accessible locations, usually on the latch side of a door, with the center of the box 48" from the floor. In a bathroom or kitchen with partially tiled walls, switches are installed at 54" to 60" to keep them above the tile. The box for a thermostat is mounted at 48" to 60". Position each box against the side of a stud so the front face will be flush with the finished wall, and drive the mounting nails into the stud.

To install a switch box between studs, first install a cross block between studs, with the top edge 46" above the floor. Position the box on the cross block so the front face will be flush with the finished wall, and drive the mounting nails into the cross block.

How to Install Electrical Boxes to Match Finished Wall Depth

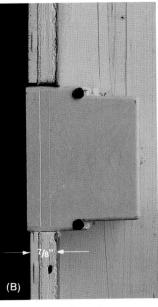

Consider the thickness of finished walls when mounting electrical boxes against framing members. Code requires that the front face of boxes be flush with the finished wall surface, so how you install boxes will vary depending on the type of wall finish that will be used. For example, if the walls will be finished with 1/2" wallboard (A), attach the boxes so the front faces extend 1/2" past the front of the framing members. With ceramic tile and wallboard (B), extend the boxes 7/8" past the framing members. With 1/4" Corian® over wallboard (C), boxes should extend 3/4"; and with wallboard and laminate (D), boxes extend 5/8".

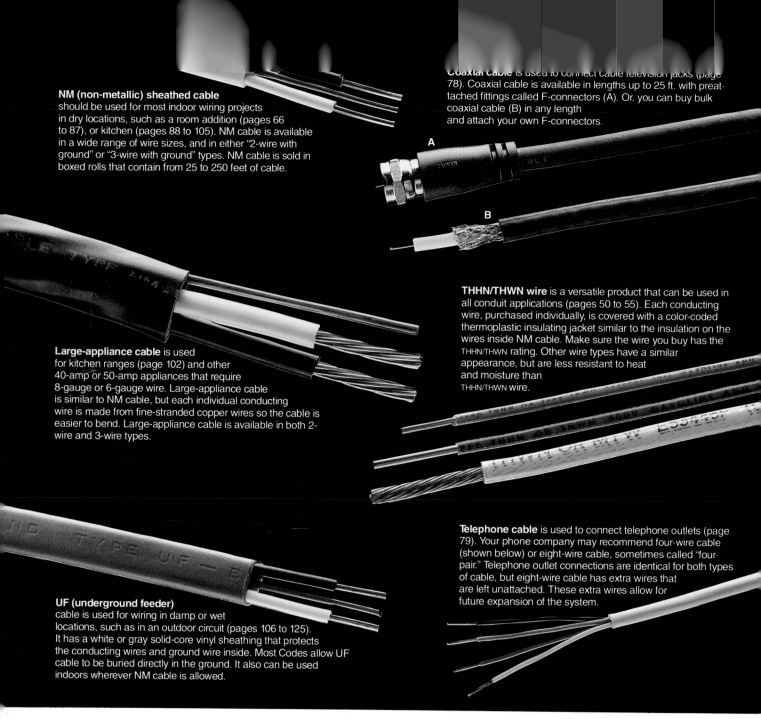

NM (non-metallic) sheathed cable
should be used for most indoor wiring projects
in dry locations, such as a room addition (pages 66
to 87), or kitchen (pages 88 to 105). NM cable is available
in a wide range of wire sizes, and in either "2-wire with
ground" or "3-wire with ground" types. NM cable is sold in
boxed rolls that contain from 25 to 250 feet of cable.

Coaxial cable is used to connect cable television jacks (page
78). Coaxial cable is available in lengths up to 25 ft. with preattached fittings called F-connectors (A). Or, you can buy bulk
coaxial cable (B) in any length
and attach your own F-connectors.

Large-appliance cable is used
for kitchen ranges (page 102) and other
40-amp or 50-amp appliances that require
8-gauge or 6-gauge wire. Large-appliance cable
is similar to NM cable, but each individual conducting
wire is made from fine-stranded copper wires so the cable is
easier to bend. Large-appliance cable is available in both 2-
wire and 3-wire types.

THHN/THWN wire is a versatile product that can be used in
all conduit applications (pages 50 to 55). Each conducting
wire, purchased individually, is covered with a color-coded
thermoplastic insulating jacket similar to the insulation on the
wires inside NM cable. Make sure the wire you buy has the
THHN/THWN rating. Other wire types have a similar
appearance, but are less resistant to heat
and moisture than
THHN/THWN wire.

UF (underground feeder)
cable is used for wiring in damp or wet
locations, such as in an outdoor circuit (pages 106 to 125).
It has a white or gray solid-core vinyl sheathing that protects
the conducting wires and ground wire inside. Most Codes allow UF
cable to be buried directly in the ground. It also can be used
indoors wherever NM cable is allowed.

Telephone cable is used to connect telephone outlets (page
79). Your phone company may recommend four-wire cable
(shown below) or eight-wire cable, sometimes called "four-
pair." Telephone outlet connections are identical for both types
of cable, but eight-wire cable has extra wires that
are left unattached. These extra wires allow for
future expansion of the system.

Wires & Cables

Many types of wire and cable are available at
home centers but only a few are used in most
home wiring projects. Check your local Electrical Code to learn which type of wire to use, and
choose wire large enough for the circuit "ampacity" (page opposite). Cables are identified
by the wire gauge and number of *insulated* circuit wires they contain. In addition, all cables
have a grounding wire. For example, a cable
labeled "12/2 W G" contains two insulated 12-
gauge wires, plus a grounding wire.

Use NM cable for new wiring installed inside
walls. NM cable is easy to install when walls
and ceilings are unfinished; these techniques
are shown throughout this book. However, some
jobs require that you run cable through finished
walls, such as when you make the feeder cable
connection linking a new circuit to the circuit-
breaker panel. Running cable in finished walls
requires extra planning, and often is easier if
you work with a helper. Sometimes cables can
be run through a finished wall by using the
gaps around a chimney or plumbing soil stack.
Other techniques for running NM cable inside
finished walls are shown on pages 48 to 49.

Tips for Working with Wire

Wire gauge		Ampacity	Maximum wattage load
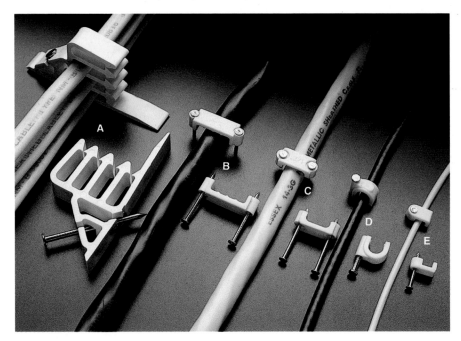	14-gauge	15 amps	1440 watts (120 volts)
	12-gauge	20 amps	1920 watts (120 volts) 3840 watts (240 volts)
	10-gauge	30 amps	2880 watts (120 volts) 5760 watts (240 volts)
	8-gauge	40 amps	7680 watts (240 volts)
	6-gauge	50 amps	9600 watts (240 volts)

Wire "ampacity" is a measurement of how much current a wire can carry safely. Ampacity varies according to the size of the wires, as shown above. When installing a new circuit , choose wire with an ampacity rating matching the circuit size. For dedicated appliance circuits, check the wattage rating of the appliance and make sure it does not exceed the maximum wattage load of the circuit.

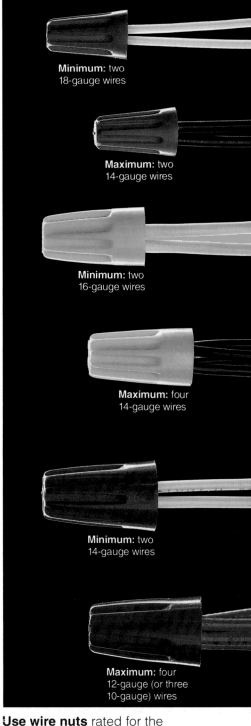

Minimum: two
18-gauge wires

Maximum: two
14-gauge wires

Minimum: two
16-gauge wires

Maximum: four
14-gauge wires

Minimum: two
14-gauge wires

Maximum: four
12-gauge (or three
10-gauge) wires

Use plastic cable staples to anchor cables to the sides of framing members. Choose staples sized to match the cables they anchor: Stack-It® staples (A) for attaching up to four 2-wire cables to the side of a framing member; 3/4" staples (B) for 12/2, 12/3, and all 10-gauge cables; 1/2" staples (C) for 14/2, 14/3, or 12/2 cables; coaxial staples (D) for anchoring television cables; bell wire staples (E) for attaching telephone cables. Cables should be anchored within 8" of each electrical box, and every 4 ft. thereafter.

Use wire nuts rated for the wires you are connecting. Wire nuts are color-coded by size, but the coding scheme varies according to manufacturer. The wire nuts shown above come from one major manufacturer. To ensure safe connections, each wire nut is rated for both minimum and maximum wire capacity. These wire nuts can be used to connect both conducting wires and grounding wires. Green wire nuts are used only for grounding wires.

Pulling cables through studs is easier if you drill smooth, straight holes at the same height. Prevent kinks by straightening the cable before pulling it through the studs.

Installing NM Cable

NM cable is used for all indoor wiring projects except those requiring conduit (see pages 50 to 55). Cut and install the cable after all electrical boxes have been mounted. Refer to your wiring plan (page 18) to make sure each length of cable is correct for the circuit size and configuration.

Cable runs are difficult to measure exactly, so leave plenty of extra wire when cutting each length. Cable splices inside walls are not allowed by Code. When inserting cables into a circuit breaker panel, **make sure the power is shut off** (page 58).

After all cables are installed, call your electrical inspector to arrange for the rough-in inspection. Do not install wallboard or attach light fixtures and other devices until this inspection is done.

Everything You Need:

Tools: drill, bits, tape measure, cable ripper, combination tool, screwdrivers, needlenose pliers, hammer.

Materials: NM cable, cable clamps, cable staples, masking tape, grounding pigtails, wire nuts.

How to Install NM Cable

1 Drill ⁵/₈" holes in framing members for the cable runs. This is done easily with a right-angle drill, available at rental centers. Holes should be set back at least 1¹/₄" from the front face of the framing members.

2 Where cables will turn corners (step 6, page opposite), drill intersecting holes in adjoining faces of studs. Measure and cut all cables, allowing 2 ft. extra at ends entering breaker panel, and 1 ft. for ends entering electrical box.

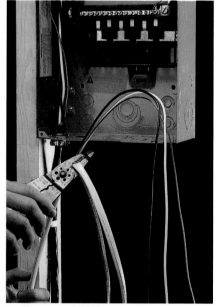

3 **Shut off power to circuit breaker panel** (page 58). Use a cable ripper to strip cable, leaving at least ¹/₄" of sheathing to enter the circuit breaker panel. Clip away the excess sheathing.

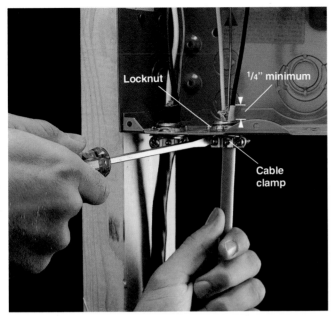

4 Open a knockout in the circuit breaker panel, using a hammer and screwdriver. Insert a cable clamp into the knockout, and secure it with a locknut. Insert the cable though the clamp so that at least 1/4" of sheathing extends inside the circuit breaker panel. Tighten the mounting screws on the clamp so the cable is gripped securely, but not so tightly that the sheathing is crushed.

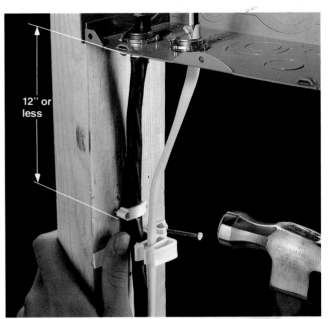

5 Anchor the cable to the center of a framing member within 12" of the circuit breaker panel, using a cable staple. Stack-It® staples work well where two or more cables must be anchored to the same side of a stud. Run the cable to the first electrical box. Where the cable runs along the sides of framing members, anchor it with cable staples no more than 4 ft. apart.

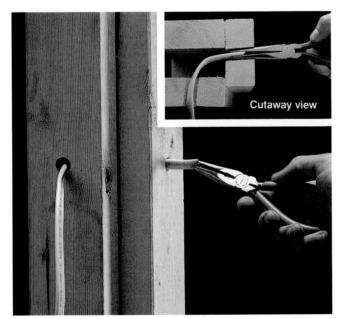

Cutaway view

6 At corners, form a slight L-shaped bend in the end of the cable and insert it into one hole. Retrieve cable through the other hole, using needlenose pliers (inset).

7 At the electrical box, staple the cable to a framing member 8" from the box. Hold the cable taut against the front of the box, and mark a point on the sheathing 1/2" past the box edge. Strip cable from the marked line to the end, using a cable ripper, and clip away excess sheathing with a combination tool. Insert the cable through the knockout in the box.

(continued next page)

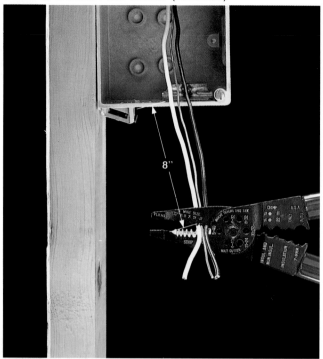

8 As each cable is installed in a box, clip back each wire so that 8" of workable wire extends past the front edge of the box.

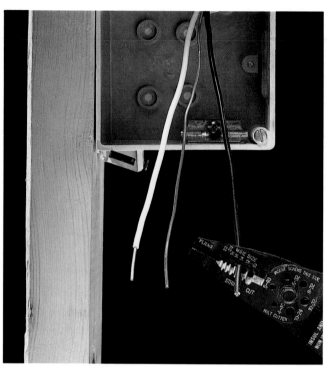

9 Strip ³/4" of insulation from each circuit wire in the box, using a combination tool. Take care not to nick the copper.

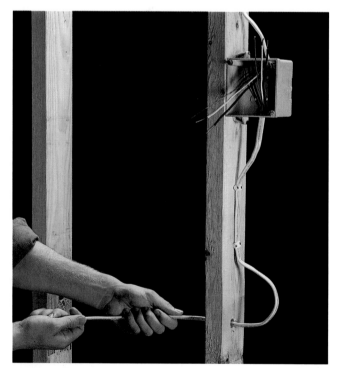

10 Continue the circuit by running cable between each pair of electrical boxes, leaving an extra 1 ft. of cable at each end.

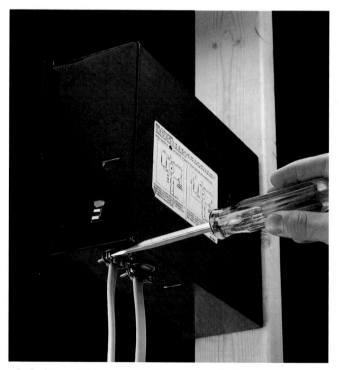

11 At metal boxes and recessed fixtures, open knockouts and attach cables with cable clamps. From inside fixture, strip away all but ¹/4" of sheathing. Clip back wires so there is 8" of workable length, then strip ³/4" of insulation from each wire.

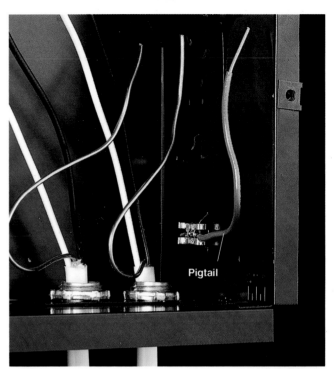

12 For a surface-mounted fixture like a baseboard heater or fluorescent light fixture, staple the cable to a stud near the fixture location, leaving plenty of excess cable. Mark the floor so the cable will be easy to find after the walls are finished.

13 At each recessed fixture and metal electrical box, connect one end of a grounding pigtail to the metal frame, using a grounding clip attached to the frame (shown above) or a green grounding screw (page 50).

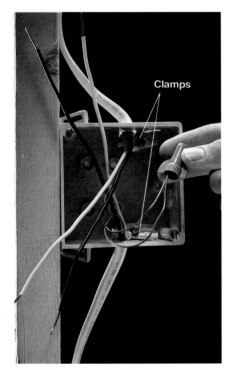

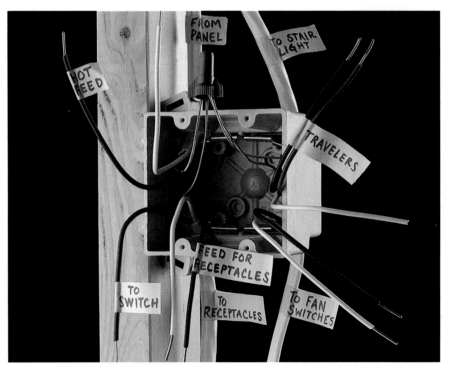

14 At each electrical box and recessed fixture, join the grounding wires together with a wire nut. If box has internal clamps, tighten the clamps over the cables.

15 Label the cables entering each box to indicate their destinations. In boxes with complex wiring configurations, also tag the individual wires to make final hookups easier. After all cables are installed, your rough-in work is ready to be reviewed by the electrical inspector.

How to Run NM Cable Inside a Finished Wall

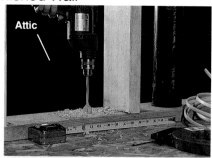

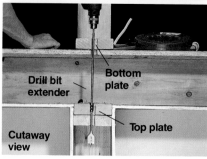

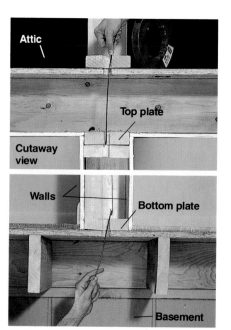

1 From the unfinished space below the finished wall, look for a reference point, like a soil stack, plumbing pipes, or electrical cables, that indicates the location of the wall above. Choose a location for the new cable that does not interfere with existing utilities. Drill a 1" hole up into the stud cavity.

2 From the unfinished space above the finished wall, find the top of the stud cavity by measuring from the same fixed reference point used in step 1. Drill a 1" hole down through the top plate and into the stud cavity, using a drill bit extender.

3 Extend a fish tape down through the top plate, twisting the tape until it reaches the bottom of the stud cavity. From the unfinished space below the wall, use a piece of stiff wire with a hook on one end to retrieve the fish tape through the drilled hole in the bottom plate.

4 Trim back 3" of outer insulation from the end of the NM cable, then insert the wires through the loop at the tip of the fish tape.

5 Bend the wires against the cable, then use electrical tape to bind them tightly. Apply cable-pulling lubricant to the taped end of the fish tape.

6 From above the finished wall, pull steadily on the fish tape to draw the cable up through the stud cavity. This job will be easier if you have a helper feed the cable from below as you pull.

Tips for Running Cable Inside Finished Walls

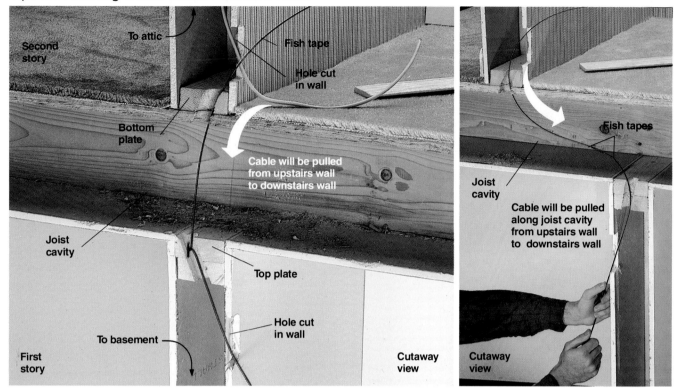

If there is no access space above and below a wall (page opposite), cut openings in the finished walls to run a cable. This often occurs in two-story homes when a cable is extended from an upstairs wall to a downstairs wall. Cut small openings in the wall near the top and bottom plates, then drill an angled 1" hole through each plate. Extend a fish tape into the joist cavity between the walls and use it to pull the cable from one wall to the next. If the walls line up one over the other (left), you can retrieve the fish tape using a piece of stiff wire. If walls do not line up (right), use a second fish tape. After running the cable, repair the holes in the walls with patching plaster, or wallboard scraps and taping compound.

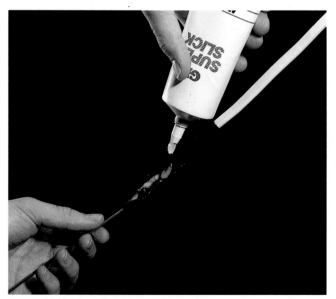

Apply cable-pulling lubricant to the taped end of the fish tape when a cable must be pulled through a sharp bend. Do not use oil or petroleum jelly as a lubricant, because they can damage the thermoplastic cable sheathing.

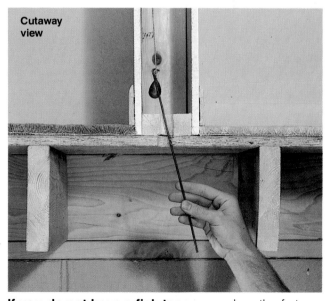

If you do not have a fish tape, use a length of sturdy mason's string and a lead fishing weight or heavy washer to fish down through a stud cavity. Drop the line into the stud cavity from above, then use a piece of stiff wire to hook the line from below.

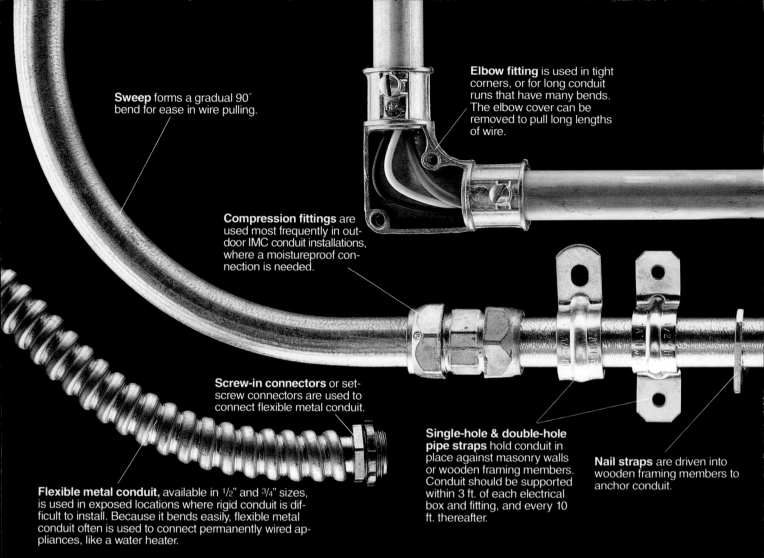

Sweep forms a gradual 90° bend for ease in wire pulling.

Elbow fitting is used in tight corners, or for long conduit runs that have many bends. The elbow cover can be removed to pull long lengths of wire.

Compression fittings are used most frequently in outdoor IMC conduit installations, where a moistureproof connection is needed.

Screw-in connectors or set-screw connectors are used to connect flexible metal conduit.

Single-hole & double-hole pipe straps hold conduit in place against masonry walls or wooden framing members. Conduit should be supported within 3 ft. of each electrical box and fitting, and every 10 ft. thereafter.

Nail straps are driven into wooden framing members to anchor conduit.

Flexible metal conduit, available in ¹/₂" and ³/₄" sizes, is used in exposed locations where rigid conduit is difficult to install. Because it bends easily, flexible metal conduit often is used to connect permanently wired appliances, like a water heater.

Conduit

Electrical wiring that runs in exposed locations must be protected by rigid tubing, called conduit. For example, conduit is used for wiring that runs across masonry walls in a basement laundry, and for exposed outdoor wiring (pages 106 to 125). THHN/THWN wire (page 42) normally is installed inside conduit, although UF or NM cable also can be installed in conduit.

There are several types of conduit available, so check with your electrical inspector to find out which type meets Code requirements in your area. Conduit installed outdoors must be rated for exterior use. Metal conduit should be used only with metal boxes, never with plastic boxes.

At one time, conduit could only be fitted by using elaborate bending techniques and special tools. Now, however, a variety of shaped fittings are available to let a homeowner join conduit easily.

Electrical Grounding in Metal Conduit

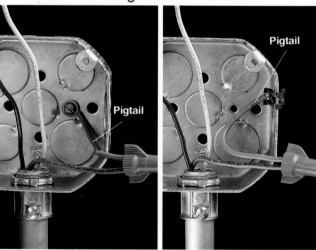

Pigtail

Pigtail

Install a green insulated grounding wire for any circuit that runs through metal conduit. Although the Code allows the metal conduit to serve as the grounding conductor, most electricians install a green insulated wire as a more dependable means of grounding the system. The grounding wires must be connected to metal boxes with a pigtail and grounding screw (left) or grounding clip (right).

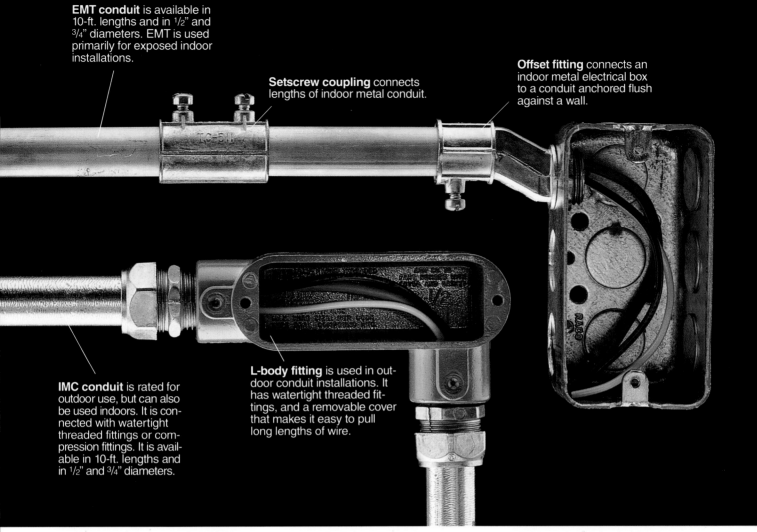

EMT conduit is available in 10-ft. lengths and in ½" and ¾" diameters. EMT is used primarily for exposed indoor installations.

Setscrew coupling connects lengths of indoor metal conduit.

Offset fitting connects an indoor metal electrical box to a conduit anchored flush against a wall.

IMC conduit is rated for outdoor use, but can also be used indoors. It is connected with watertight threaded fittings or compression fittings. It is available in 10-ft. lengths and in ½" and ¾" diameters.

L-body fitting is used in outdoor conduit installations. It has watertight threaded fittings, and a removable cover that makes it easy to pull long lengths of wire.

Wire Capacities of Conduit

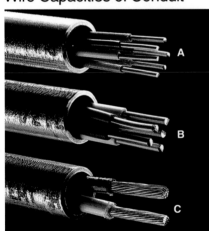

Conduit ½" in diameter can hold up to six 14-gauge or 12-gauge THHN/THWN wires (A), five 10-gauge wires (B), or two 8-gauge wires (C). Use ¾" conduit if the number of wires exceeds this capacity.

Three Metal Conduit Variations

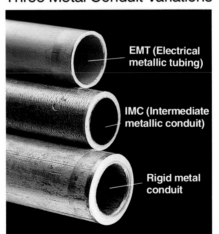

EMT (Electrical metallic tubing)

IMC (Intermediate metallic conduit)

Rigid metal conduit

EMT is lightweight and easy to install, but should not be used where it can be damaged. IMC has thicker, galvanized walls and is a good choice for exposed outdoor use. Rigid metal conduit provides the greatest protection for wires, but is more expensive and requires threaded fittings.

Plastic Conduit Variation

Plastic PVC conduit is allowed by many local Codes. It is assembled with solvent glue and PVC fittings that resemble those for metal conduit. PVC conduit should be attached only to PVC boxes, never to metal boxes. When wiring with PVC conduit, always run a green grounding wire.

How to Install Metal Conduit & THHN/THWN Wire on Masonry Walls

  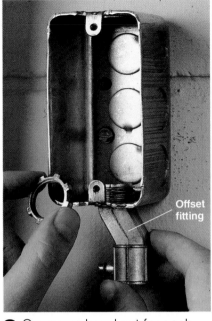

1 Measure from floor to position electrical boxes on wall, and mark location for mounting screws. Boxes for receptacles in an unfinished basement or other damp area are mounted at least 2 ft. from the floor. Laundry receptacles usually are mounted at 48".

2 Drill pilot holes with a masonry bit, then mount the boxes against masonry walls with Tapcon® anchors. Or, use masonry anchors and pan-head screws.

3 Open one knockout for each length of conduit that will be attached to the box. Attach an offset fitting to each knockout, using a locknut.

Offset fitting

4 Measure the first length of conduit and cut it with a hacksaw. Remove any rough inside edges with a pipe reamer or a round file. Attach the conduit to the offset fitting on the box, and tighten the setscrew.

5 Anchor the conduit against the wall with pipe straps and Tapcon® anchors. Conduit should be anchored within 3 ft. of each box and fitting, and every 10 ft. thereafter.

6 Make conduit bends by attaching a sweep fitting, using a setscrew fitting or compression fitting. Continue conduit run by attaching additional lengths, using setscrew or compression fittings.

7 Use an elbow fitting in conduit runs that have many bends, or runs that require very long wires. The cover on the elbow fitting can be removed to make it easier to extend a fish tape and pull wires.

8 At the service breaker panel, **turn the power OFF, then remove the cover and test for power** (page 58). Open a knock-out in the panel, then attach a set-screw fitting and install the last length of conduit.

9 Unwind the fish tape and extend it through the conduit from the circuit breaker panel outward. Remove the cover on an elbow fitting when extending the fish tape around tight corners.

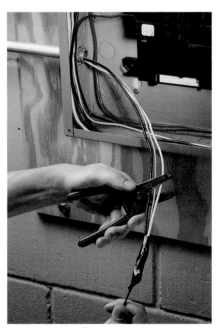

10 Insert the wires through the loop at the end of the fish tape, and wrap them with electrical tape. Straighten the wires to prevent kinks, and apply wire-pulling lubricant to the taped end of the fish tape.

11 Retrieve the wires through the conduit by pulling on the fish tape with steady pressure. **NOTE: Use extreme care** when using a metal fish tape inside a circuit breaker panel, even when the power is turned OFF.

12 Clip off the taped ends of the wires. Leave at least 2 ft. of wire at the service panel, and 8" at each electrical box.

Wiring a Laundry with Conduit

A typical home laundry has three electrical circuits. A 20-amp, 120-volt small-appliance circuit wired with 12-gauge THHN/THWN wire supplies power for the washing machine receptacle and all other general-use receptacles in the laundry area. A basic lighting circuit, often extended from another part of the house, powers the laundry light fixture. Finally, a 240-volt, 30-amp circuit wired with 10-gauge THHN/THWN wire provides power for the dryer.

Follow the directions on pages 52 to 53 when installing the conduit. For convenience, you can use the same conduit to hold the wires for both the 120-volt circuit and the 240-volt dryer circuit.

Everything You Need:

Tools: hacksaw, drill and 1/8" masonry bit, screwdriver, fish tape, combination tool.

Materials: conduit, setscrew fittings, Tapcon® anchors, THHN/THWN wire, electrical tape, wire nuts, receptacles (GFCI, 120-volt, 120/240-volt), circuit breakers (30-amp double-pole, 20-amp single-pole).

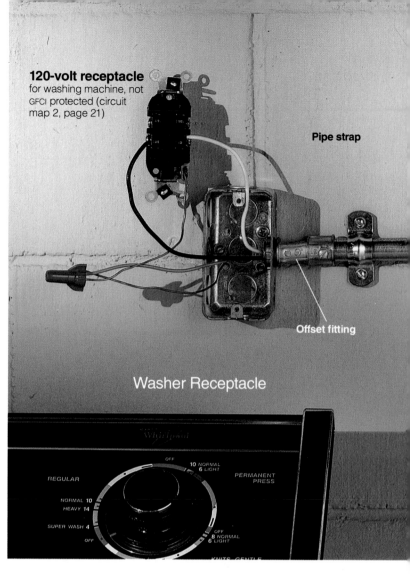

120-volt receptacle for washing machine, not GFCI protected (circuit map 2, page 21)

Pipe strap

Offset fitting

Washer Receptacle

How to Connect a 30-amp Dryer Circuit (conduit installation)

1 Connect the white circuit wire to the center setscrew terminal on the receptacle. Connect the black and red wires to the remaining setscrew terminals, and connect the green insulated wire to the grounding screw in the box. Attach the coverplate.

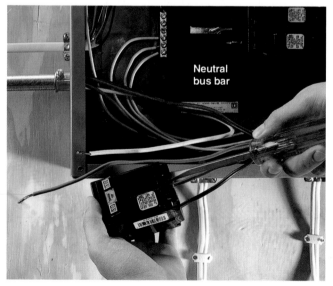

Neutral bus bar

2 With main breaker shut OFF, connect the red and black circuit wires to the setscrew terminals on the 30-amp double-pole breaker. Connect the white wire to the neutral bus bar. Attach the green insulated wire to the grounding bus bar. Attach the breaker panel cover, and turn the breakers ON.

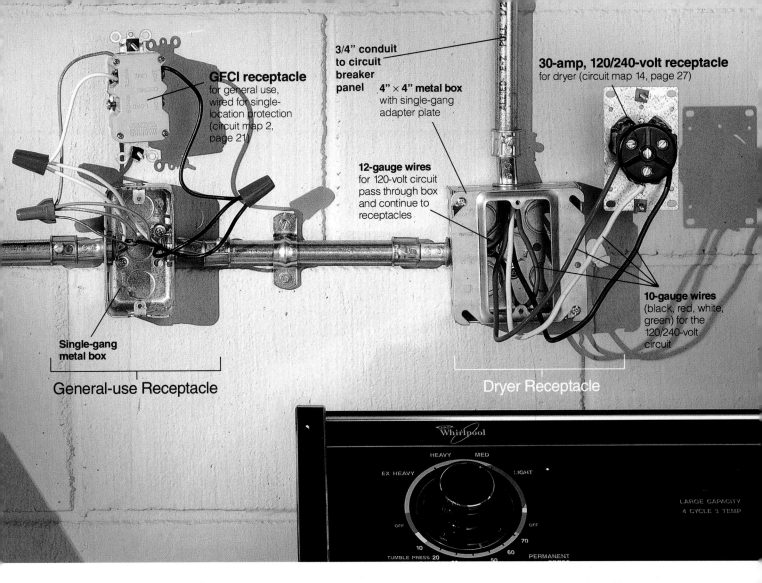

GFCI receptacle
for general use, wired for single-location protection (circuit map 2, page 21)

3/4" conduit to circuit breaker panel

4" × 4" metal box with single-gang adapter plate

30-amp, 120/240-volt receptacle for dryer (circuit map 14, page 27)

12-gauge wires for 120-volt circuit pass through box and continue to receptacles

10-gauge wires (black, red, white, green) for the 120/240-volt circuit

Single-gang metal box

General-use Receptacle

Dryer Receptacle

Whirlpool

Wiring a Water Heater with Flexible Conduit

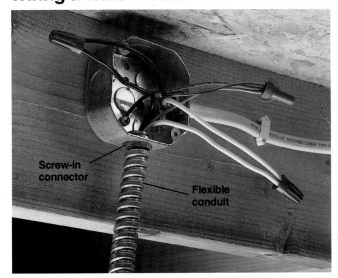

Screw-in connector

Flexible conduit

Install a 30-amp, 240-volt circuit for most electric water heaters. A water heater circuit is wired in much the same way as an air conditioner circuit (circuit map 12, page 26). Install a junction box near the water heater, then use 10/2 NM cable to bring power from the service panel to the junction box (above left).

Use flexible metal conduit and 10-gauge THHN/THWN wires to bring power from the junction box to the water heater wire connection box (above right). Connect black and red water heater leads to the white and black circuit wires. Connect the grounding wire to the water heater grounding screw .

Circuit Breaker Panels

The circuit breaker panel is the electrical distribution center for your home. It divides the current into branch circuits that are carried throughout the house. Each branch circuit is controlled by a circuit breaker that protects the wires from dangerous current overloads. When installing new circuits, the last step is to connect the wires to new circuit breakers at the panel. Working inside a circuit breaker panel is not dangerous if you follow basic safety procedures. Always shut off the main circuit breaker and test for power

before touching any parts inside the panel, and **never touch the service wire lugs.** If unsure of your own skills, hire an electrician to make the final circuit connections. (If you have an older electrical service with fuses instead of circuit breakers, always have an electrician make these final hookups.)

If the main circuit breaker panel does not have enough open slots to hold new circuit breakers, install a subpanel (pages 60 to 63). This job is well within the skill level of an experienced do-it-

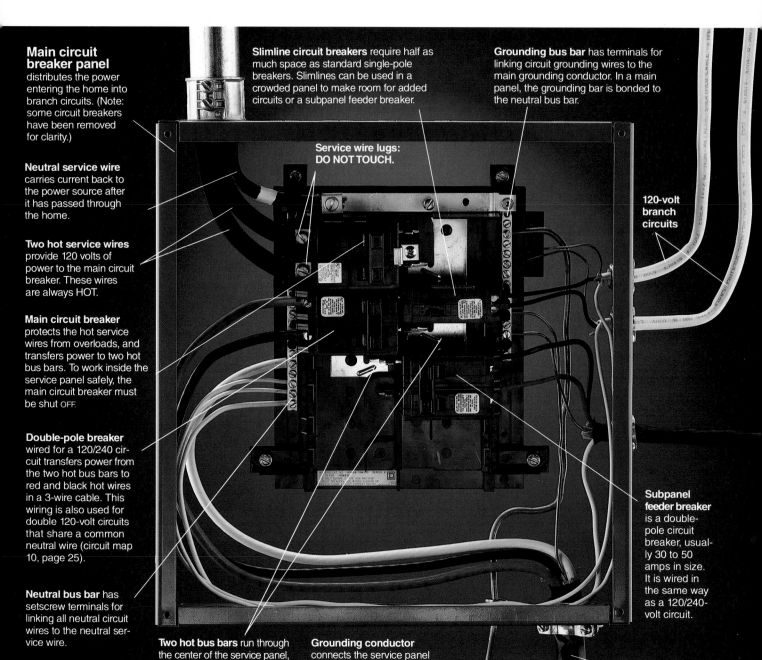

Main circuit breaker panel distributes the power entering the home into branch circuits. (Note: some circuit breakers have been removed for clarity.)

Neutral service wire carries current back to the power source after it has passed through the home.

Two hot service wires provide 120 volts of power to the main circuit breaker. These wires are always HOT.

Main circuit breaker protects the hot service wires from overloads, and transfers power to two hot bus bars. To work inside the service panel safely, the main circuit breaker must be shut OFF.

Double-pole breaker wired for a 120/240 circuit transfers power from the two hot bus bars to red and black hot wires in a 3-wire cable. This wiring is also used for double 120-volt circuits that share a common neutral wire (circuit map 10, page 25).

Neutral bus bar has setscrew terminals for linking all neutral circuit wires to the neutral service wire.

Slimline circuit breakers require half as much space as standard single-pole breakers. Slimlines can be used in a crowded panel to make room for added circuits or a subpanel feeder breaker.

Service wire lugs: **DO NOT TOUCH.**

Grounding bus bar has terminals for linking circuit grounding wires to the main grounding conductor. In a main panel, the grounding bar is bonded to the neutral bus bar.

120-volt branch circuits

Subpanel feeder breaker is a double-pole circuit breaker, usually 30 to 50 amps in size. It is wired in the same way as a 120/240-volt circuit.

Two hot bus bars run through the center of the service panel, supplying power to the individual circuit breakers. Each carries 120 volts of power.

Grounding conductor connects the service panel equipment to a metal cold water pipe or grounding rod driven into the earth.

120/240-volt branch circuit

yourselfer, although you can also hire an electrician to install the subpanel.

Before installing any new wiring, evaluate your electrical service to make sure it provides enough current to support both the existing wiring and any new circuits (pages 14 to 17). If your service does not provide enough power, have an electrician upgrade it to a higher amp rating. During the upgrade, the electrician will install a new circuit breaker panel with

enough extra breaker slots for the new circuits you want to install.

Safety Warning:

Never touch any parts inside a circuit breaker panel until you have checked for power (page 58). Circuit breaker panels differ in appearance, depending on the manufacturer. Never begin work in a circuit breaker panel until you understand its layout and can identify the parts.

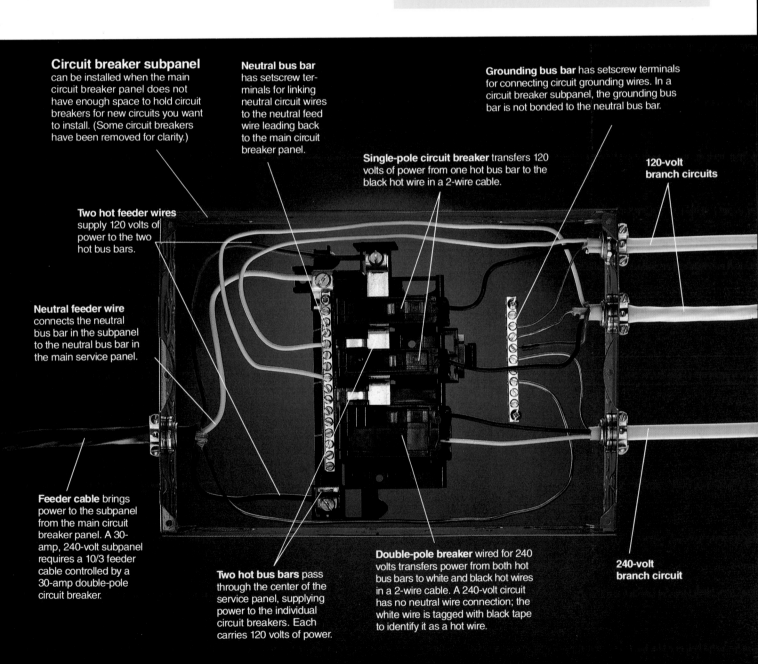

Circuit breaker subpanel can be installed when the main circuit breaker panel does not have enough space to hold circuit breakers for new circuits you want to install. (Some circuit breakers have been removed for clarity.)

Neutral bus bar has setscrew terminals for linking neutral circuit wires to the neutral feed wire leading back to the main circuit breaker panel.

Grounding bus bar has setscrew terminals for connecting circuit grounding wires. In a circuit breaker subpanel, the grounding bus bar is not bonded to the neutral bus bar.

Single-pole circuit breaker transfers 120 volts of power from one hot bus bar to the black hot wire in a 2-wire cable.

120-volt branch circuits

Two hot feeder wires supply 120 volts of power to the two hot bus bars.

Neutral feeder wire connects the neutral bus bar in the subpanel to the neutral bus bar in the main service panel.

Feeder cable brings power to the subpanel from the main circuit breaker panel. A 30-amp, 240-volt subpanel requires a 10/3 feeder cable controlled by a 30-amp double-pole circuit breaker.

Two hot bus bars pass through the center of the service panel, supplying power to the individual circuit breakers. Each carries 120 volts of power.

Double-pole breaker wired for 240 volts transfers power from both hot bus bars to white and black hot wires in a 2-wire cable. A 240-volt circuit has no neutral wire connection; the white wire is tagged with black tape to identify it as a hot wire.

240-volt branch circuit

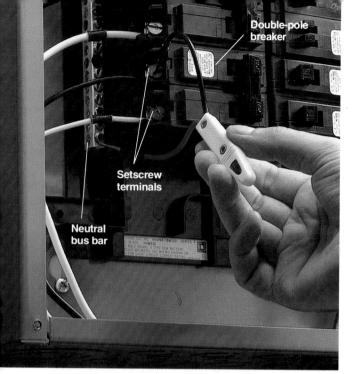

Double-pole breaker

Setscrew terminals

Neutral bus bar

Test for current before touching any parts inside a circuit breaker panel. With main breaker turned OFF but all other breakers turned ON, touch one probe of a neon tester to the neutral bus bar, and touch other probe to each setscrew on one of the double-pole breakers (not the main breaker). If tester does not light for either setscrew, it is safe to work in the panel.

Connecting Circuit Breakers

The last step in a wiring project is connecting circuits at the breaker panel. After this is done, the work is ready for the final inspection.

Circuits are connected at the main breaker panel, if it has enough open slots, or at a circuit breaker subpanel (pages 60 to 63). When working at a subpanel, make sure the feeder breaker at the main panel has been turned OFF, and test for power (photo, left) before touching any parts in the subpanel.

Make sure the circuit breaker amperage does not exceed the "ampacity" of the circuit wires you are connecting to it (page 43). Also be aware that circuit breaker styles and installation techniques vary according to manufacturer. Use breakers designed for your type of panel.

Everything You Need:

Tools: screwdriver, hammer, pencil, combination tool, cable ripper, neon circuit tester, pliers.

Materials: cable clamps, single- and double-pole circuit breakers.

How to Connect Circuit Breakers

1 Shut off the main circuit breaker in the main circuit breaker panel (if you are working in a subpanel, shut off the feeder breaker in the main panel). Remove the panel coverplate, taking care not to touch the parts inside the panel. Test for power (photo, above).

2 Open a knockout in the side of the circuit breaker panel, using a screwdriver and hammer. Attach a cable clamp to the knockout.

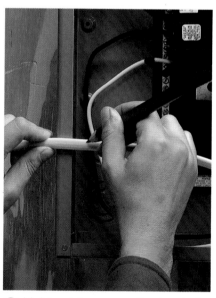

3 Hold cable across the front of the panel near the knockout, and mark sheathing about 1/2" inside the edge of the panel. Strip the cable from marked line to end, using a cable ripper. (There should be 18" to 24" of excess cable.) Insert the cable through the clamp and into the service panel, then tighten the clamp.

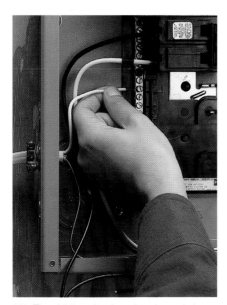

4 Bend the bare copper grounding wire around the inside edge of the panel to an open setscrew terminal on the grounding bus bar. Insert the wire into the opening on the bus bar, and tighten the setscrew. Fold excess wire around the inside edge of the panel.

5 For 120-volt circuits, bend the white circuit wire around the outside of the panel to an open setscrew terminal on the neutral bus bar. Clip away excess wire, then strip 1/2" of insulation from the wire, using a combination tool. Insert the wire into the terminal opening, and tighten the setscrew.

6 Strip 1/2" of insulation from the end of the black circuit wire. Insert the wire into the setscrew terminal on a new single-pole circuit breaker, and tighten the setscrew.

7 Slide one end of the circuit breaker onto the guide hook, then press it firmly against the bus bar until it snaps into place. (Breaker installation may vary, depending on the manufacturer.) Fold excess black wire around the inside edge of the panel.

8 **120/240-volt circuits (top):** Connect red and black wires to double-pole breaker. Connect white wire to neutral bus bar, and grounding wire to grounding bus bar. **240-volt circuits (bottom):** Attach white and black wires to double-pole breaker, tagging white wire with black tape. There is no neutral bus bar connection on this circuit.

9 Remove the appropriate breaker knockout on the panel coverplate to make room for the new circuit breaker. A single-pole breaker requires one knockout, while a double-pole breaker requires two knockouts. Reattach the coverplate, and label the new circuit on the panel index.

Before

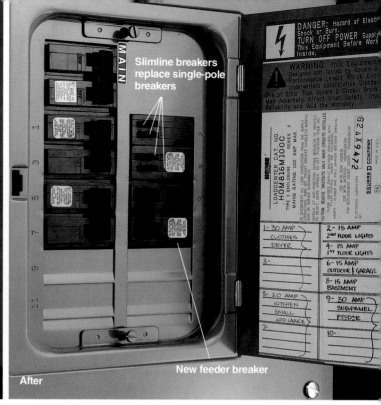

After

If there are no open circuit breaker slots in the main circuit breaker panel (above, left), you can make room for a subpanel feeder breaker by replacing some of the single-pole breakers with slimline breakers (above, right). Slimline breakers take up half the space of standard breakers, allowing you to fit two circuits into one single slot on the service

panel. In the service panel shown above, four single-pole 120-volt breakers were replaced with slimline breakers to provide the double opening needed for a 30-amp, 240-volt subpanel feeder breaker. Use slimline breakers with the same amp rating as the standard single-pole breakers you are removing and make sure they are approved for use in your panel.

Installing a Subpanel

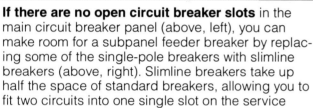

Install a circuit breaker subpanel if the main circuit breaker panel does not have enough open breaker slots for the new circuits you are planning. The subpanel serves as a second distribution center for connecting circuits. It receives power from a double-pole "feeder" circuit breaker you install in the main circuit breaker panel.

If the main service panel is so full that there is no room for the double-pole subpanel feeder breaker, you can reconnect some of the existing 120-volt circuits to special slimline breakers (photos, above).

Plan your subpanel installation carefully (page opposite), making sure your electrical service supplies enough power to support the extra load of the new subpanel circuits. Assuming your main service is adequate, consider installing an oversized subpanel feeder breaker in the main panel to provide enough extra amps to meet the needs of future wiring projects.

Also consider the physical size of the subpanel, and choose one that has enough extra slots to

hold circuits you may want to install later. The smallest panels have room for up to 6 single-pole breakers (or 3 double-pole breakers), while the largest models can hold up to 20 single-pole breakers.

Subpanels often are mounted near the main circuit breaker panel. Or, for convenience, they can be installed close to the areas they serve, such as in a new room addition or a garage. In a finished room, a subpanel can be painted or covered with a removable painting, bulletin board, or decorative cabinet to make it more attractive. If it is covered, make sure the subpanel is easily accessible and clearly identified.

Everything You Need:

Tools: hammer, screwdriver, neon circuit tester, cable ripper, combination tool.

Materials: screws, cable clamps, 3-wire NM cable, cable staples, double-pole circuit breaker, circuit breaker subpanel, slimline circuit breakers

How to Plan a Subpanel Installation (photocopy this work sheet as a guide; blue sample numbers will not reproduce)

1. Find the gross electrical load for only those areas that will be served by the subpanel. Refer to "Evaluating Electrical Loads" (steps 1 to 5, page 17). EXAMPLE: In the 400-sq. ft. attic room addition shown on pages 66 to 69, the gross load required for the basic lighting/receptacle circuits and electric heating is 5000 watts.	Gross Electrical Load:	_5000_ watts
2. Multiply the gross electrical load times 1.25. This safety adjustment is required by the National Electrical Code. EXAMPLE: In the attic room addition (gross load 5000 watts), the adjusted load equals 6250 watts.	_5000_ watts × 1.25 =	_6250_ watts
3. Convert the load into amps by dividing by 230. This gives the required amperage needed to power the subpanel. EXAMPLE: The attic room addition described above requires about 27 amps of power (6250 ÷ 230).	_6,250_ watts ÷ 230 =	_27.2_ amps
4. For the subpanel feeder breaker, choose a double-pole circuit breaker with an amp rating equal to or greater than the required subpanel amperage. EXAMPLE: In a room addition that requires 27 amps, choose a 30-amp double-pole feeder breaker.	☑ 30-amp breaker ☐ 40-amp breaker ☐ 50-amp breaker	
5. For the feeder cable bringing power from the main circuit breaker panel to the subpanel, choose 3-wire NM cable with an ampacity equal to the rating of the subpanel feeder breaker (see page 43). EXAMPLE: For a 30-amp subpanel feeder breaker, choose 10/3 cable for the feeder.	☑ 10/3 cable ☐ 8/3 cable ☐ 6/3 cable	

How to Install a Subpanel

1 Mount the subpanel at shoulder height, following manufacturer's recommendations. The subpanel can be mounted to the sides of studs, or to plywood attached between two studs. Panel shown here extends 1/2" past the face of studs so it will be flush with the finished wall surface.

2 Open a knockout in the subpanel, using a screwdriver and hammer. Run the feeder cable from the main circuit breaker panel to the subpanel, leaving about 2 ft. of excess cable at each end. See pages 48 to 49 if you need to run the cable through finished walls.

3 Attach a cable clamp to the knockout in the subpanel. Insert the cable into the subpanel, then anchor it to framing members within 8" of each panel, and every 4 ft. thereafter.

(continued next page)

How to Install a Subpanel (continued)

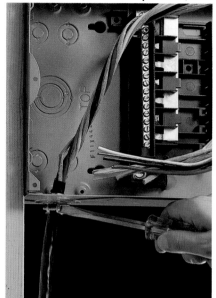

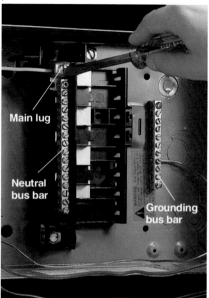

4 Strip away outer sheathing from the feeder cable, using a cable ripper. Leave at least 1/4" of sheathing extending into the subpanel. Tighten the cable clamp screws so cable is held securely, but not so tightly that the wire sheathing is crushed.

5 Strip 1/2" of insulation from the white neutral feeder wire, and attach it to the main lug on the subpanel neutral bus bar. Connect the grounding wire to a setscrew terminal on the grounding bus bar. Fold excess wire around the inside edge of the subpanel.

6 Strip away 1/2" of insulation from the red and black feeder wires. Attach one wire to the main lug on each of the hot bus bars. Fold excess wire around the inside edge of the subpanel.

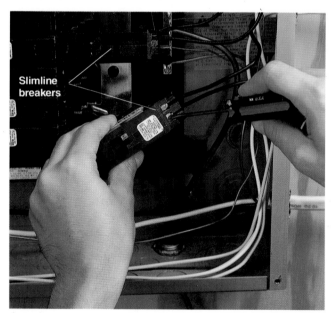

7 At the main circuit breaker panel, shut off the main circuit breaker, then remove the coverplate and test for power (page 58). If necessary, make room for the double-pole feeder breaker by removing single-pole breakers and reconnecting the wires to slimline circuit breakers. Open a knockout for the feeder cable, using a hammer and screwdriver.

8 Strip away the outer sheathing from the feeder cable so that at least 1/4" of sheathing will reach into the main service panel. Attach a cable clamp to the cable, then insert the cable into the knockout and anchor it by threading a locknut onto the clamp. Tighten the locknut by driving a screwdriver against the lugs. Tighten the clamp screws so cable is held securely, but not so tightly that the cable sheathing is crushed.

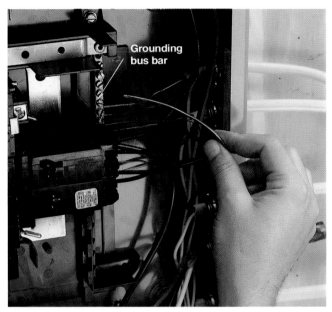

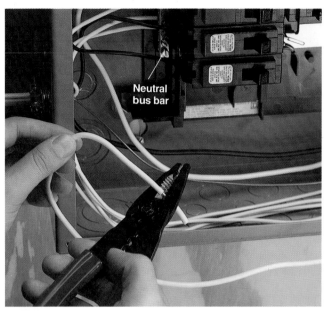

9 Bend the bare copper wire from the feeder cable around the inside edge of the main circuit breaker panel, and connect it to one of the setscrew terminals on the grounding bus bar.

10 Strip away 1/2" of insulation from the white feeder wire. Attach the wire to one of the setscrew terminals on the neutral bus bar. Fold excess wire around the inside edge of the service panel.

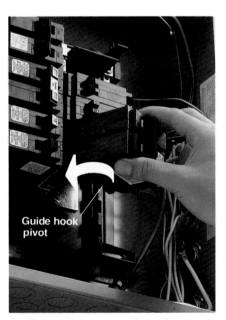

11 Strip 1/2" of insulation from the red and black feeder wires. Attach one wire to each of the setscrew terminals on the double-pole feeder breaker.

12 Hook the end of the feeder circuit breaker over the guide hooks on the panel, then push the other end forward until the breaker snaps onto the hot bus bars (follow manufacturer's directions). Fold excess wire around the inside edge of the circuit breaker panel.

13 If necessary, open two knockouts where the double-pole feeder breaker will fit, then reattach the coverplate. Label the feeder breaker on the circuit index. Turn main breaker ON, but leave feeder breaker OFF until all subpanel circuits have been connected and inspected.

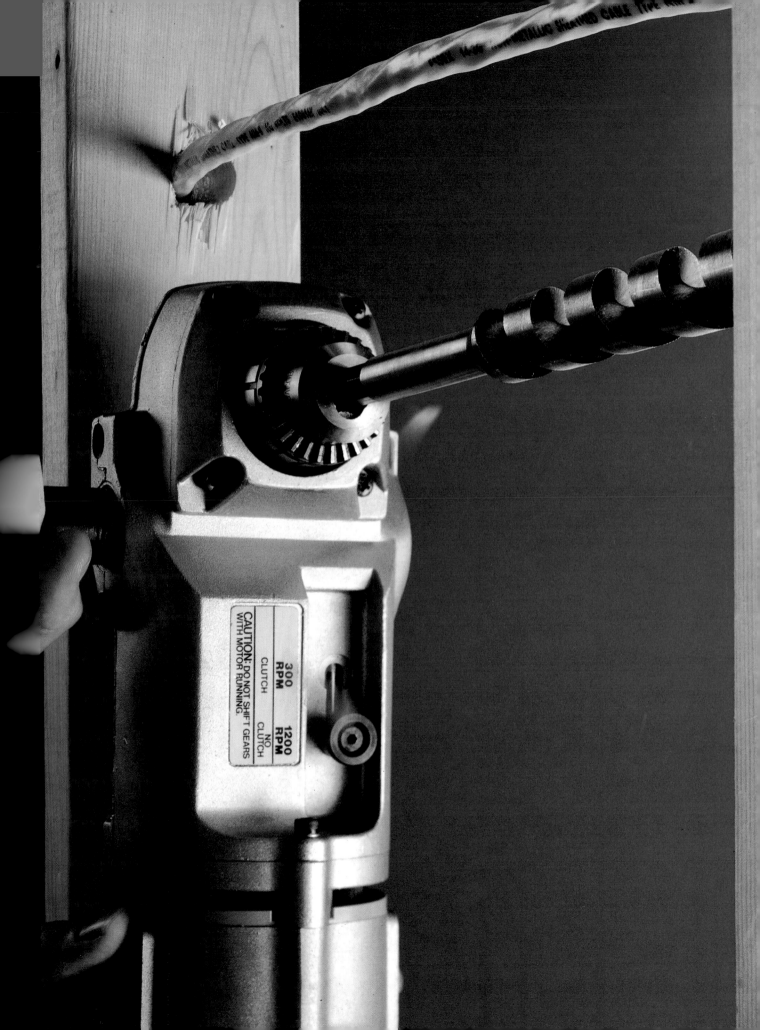

CAUTION: DO NOT SHIFT GEARS
WITH MOTOR RUNNING.

300 RPM	1200 RPM
CLUTCH	NO CLUTCH

Advanced Wiring Projects

Wiring a Room Addition

This chapter shows how to wire an unfinished attic space that is being converted to a combination bedroom, bathroom, and study. In addition to basic receptacles and light fixtures, you will learn how to install a ceiling fan, permanent- ly wired smoke alarm, bathroom vent fan, computer receptacle, air-conditioning receptacle, electric heaters, telephone outlets, and cable television jacks. Use this chapter and the circuit maps on pages 21 to 31 as a guide for planning

Choose the Fixtures You Need

A: Computer receptacle (circuit #2) is connected to a 120-volt isolated-ground circuit. It protects sensitive computer equipment from power surges. See page 82.

B: Air-conditioner receptacle (circuit # 3) supplies power for a 240-volt window air conditioner. See page 82. Some air conditioners require 120-volt receptacles.

C: Circuit breaker subpanel controls all attic circuits and fixtures, and is connected to the main service panel. For a more finished appearance, cover the subpanel with a removable bulletin board or picture. See pages 60 to 63.

D: Thermostat (circuit #5) controls 240-volt baseboard heaters in the bedroom and study areas. See page 86.

E: Fully wired bathroom (circuit #1) includes vent fan with timer switch, GFCI receptacle, vanity light, and single-pole switch. See pages 80 to 81. The bathroom also has a 240-volt blower-heater controlled by a built-in thermostat (circuit #5, page 86).

F: Closet light fixture (circuit #1) makes a closet more convenient. See page 81.

G: Smoke alarm (circuit #4) is an essential safety feature of any sleeping area. See page 85.

and installing your own circuits. Our room addition features a circuit breaker subpanel that has been installed in the attic to provide power for five new electrical circuits. Turn the page to see how these circuits look inside the walls.

Three Steps for Wiring a Room Addition
1. Plan the Circuits (pages 72 to 73).
2. Install Boxes & Cables (pages 74 to 79).
3. Make Final Connections (pages 80 to 87).

H: Double-gang switch box (circuit #4) contains a three-way switch that controls stairway light fixture and single-pole switch that controls a switched receptacle in the bedroom area. See page 83.

I: Fan switches (circuit #4) include a speed control for ceiling fan motor and dimmer control for the fan light fixture. See page 83.

J: Ceiling fan (circuit #4) helps reduce summer cooling costs and winter heating bills. See page 84.

K: Stairway light (circuit #4) illuminates the stairway. It is controlled by three-way switches at the top and bottom of the stairway. See page 85.

L: Cable television jack completes the bedroom entertainment corner. See page 78.

M: Telephone outlet is a convenient addition to the bedroom area. See page 79.

N: Switched receptacle (circuit #4) lets you turn a table lamp on from a switch at the stairway. See page 84.

O: Receptacles (circuit #4) spaced at regular intervals allow you to plug in lamps and small appliances wherever needed. See page 84.

P: Baseboard heaters (circuit #5) connected to a 240-volt circuit provide safe, effective heating. See page 87.

Wiring a Room Addition: Construction View

The room addition wiring project on the following pages includes the installation of five new electrical circuits: two 120-volt basic lighting/receptacle circuits, a dedicated 120-volt circuit with a special "isolated" grounding connection for a home computer, and two 240-volt circuits for air conditioning and heaters. The photo below shows how these circuits look behind the finished walls of a room addition.

Learn How to Install These Circuits & Cables

■ **#1: Bathroom circuit.** This 15-amp, 120-volt circuit supplies power to bathroom fixtures and to fixtures in the adjacent closet. All general-use receptacles in a bathroom must be protected by a GFCI.

■ **#2: Computer circuit.** A 15-amp, 120-volt dedicated circuit with an extra isolated grounding wire that protects computer equipment.

Circuit breaker subpanel receives power through a 10-gauge, three-wire feeder cable connected to a 30-amp, 240-volt circuit breaker at the main circuit breaker panel. Larger room additions may require a 40-amp or a 50-amp "feeder" circuit breaker.

■ **#3: Air-conditioner circuit.** A 20-amp, 240-volt dedicated circuit. In cooler climates, or in a smaller room, you may need an air conditioner and circuit rated for only 120 volts (page 13).

Wiring a room addition is a complex project that is made simple by careful planning and a step-by-step approach. Divide the project into convenient steps, and complete the work for each step before moving on to the next.

14/3 cable

14/3 cable

Phone cable

Coaxial cable

These cables continue through the foreground wall to complete the circuits. This wall has been removed for clarity.

12/2 cable

14/2 cable

■ **#4: Basic lighting/ receptacle circuit.** This 15-amp, 120-volt circuit supplies power to most of the fixtures in the bedroom and study areas.

■ **#5: Heater circuit.** This 20-amp, 240-volt circuit supplies power to the bathroom blower-heater and to the baseboard heaters. Depending on the size of your room and the wattage rating of the baseboard heaters, you may need a 30-amp, 240-volt heating circuit.

Telephone outlet is wired with 22-gauge four-wire phone cable. If your home phone system has two or more separate lines, you may need to run a cable with eight wires, commonly called "four-pair" cable.

Cable television jack is wired with coaxial cable running from an existing television junction in the utility area.

Wiring a Room Addition: Diagram View

This diagram view shows the layout of five circuits and the location of the switches, receptacles, lights, and other fixtures in the attic room addition featured in this chapter. The size and number of circuits, and the list of required materials, are based on the needs of this

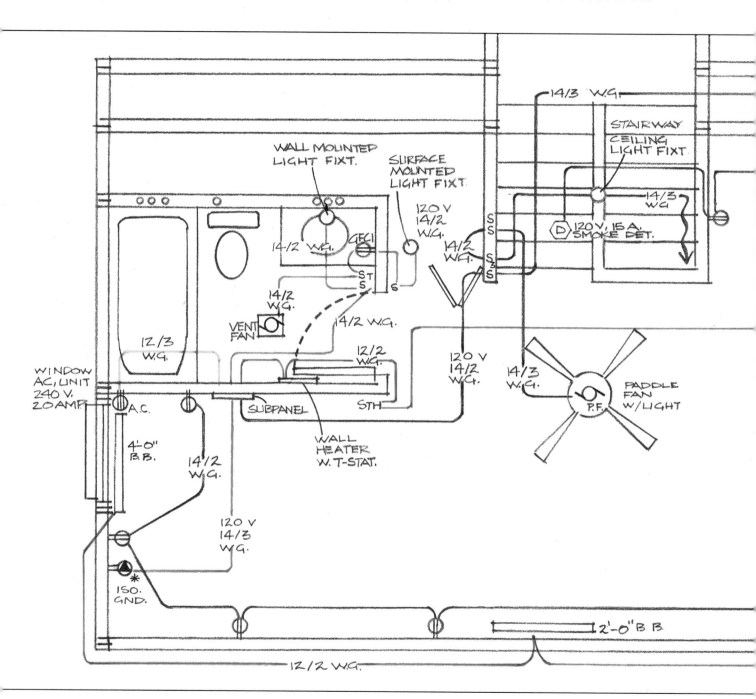

■ **Circuit #1:** A 15-amp, 120-volt circuit serving the bathroom and closet area. 14/2 NM cable, double-gang box, timer switch, single-pole switch, 4" × 4" box with single-gang adapter plate, GFCI receptacle, 2 plastic light fixture boxes, vanity light fixture, closet light fixture, 15-amp single-pole circuit breaker.

■ **Circuit #2:** A 15-amp, 120-volt computer circuit. 14/3 NM cable, single-gang box, 15-amp isolated-ground receptacle, 15-amp single-pole circuit breaker.

400-sq. ft. space. No two room additions are alike, so you will need to create a separate wiring diagram to serve as a guide for your own wiring project.

Note:
See pages 18 to 19 for a key to the common electrical symbols used in this diagram, and to learn how to draw your own wiring diagrams.

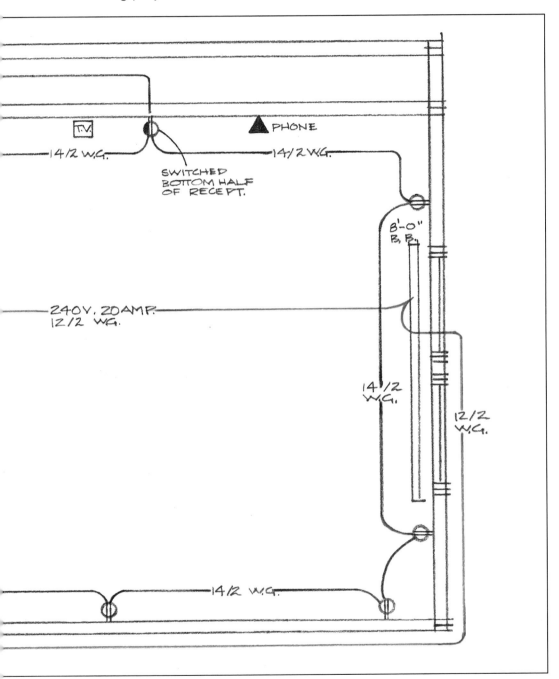

▶ **Telephone outlet:** 22-gauge four-wire phone cable (or eight-wire cable, if required by your telephone company), flush-mount telephone outlet.

TV **Cable television jack:** coaxial cable with F-connectors, signal splitter, cable television outlet with mounting brackets.

■ **Circuit #5 :** A 20-amp, 240-volt circuit that supplies power to three baseboard heaters controlled by a wall thermostat, and to a bathroom blower-heater controlled by a built-in thermostat. 12/2 NM cable, 750-watt blower-heater, single-gang box, line-voltage thermostat, three baseboard heaters, 20-amp double-pole circuit breaker.

Circuit #3: A 20-amp, 240-volt air-conditioner circuit. 12/2 NM cable; single-gang box; 20-amp, 240-volt receptacle (duplex or singleplex style); 20-amp double-pole circuit.

■ **Circuit #4 :** A 15-amp, 120-volt basic lighting/receptacle circuit serving most of the fixtures in the bedroom and study areas. 14/2 and 14/3 NM cable, 2 double-gang boxes, fan speed-control switch, dimmer switch, single-pole switch, 2 three-way switches, 2 plastic light fixture boxes, light fixture for stairway, smoke detector, metal light fixture box with brace bar, ceiling fan with light fixture, 10 single-gang boxes, 4" × 4" box with single-gang adapter plate, 10 duplex receptacles (15-amp), 15-amp single-pole circuit breaker.

1: Plan the Circuits

Your plans for wiring a room addition should reflect how you will use the space. For example, an attic space used as a bedroom requires an air-conditioner circuit, while a basement area used as a sewing room needs extra lighting. See pages 6 to 13 for information on planning circuits, and call or visit your city building inspector's office to learn the local Code requirements. You will need to create a detailed wiring diagram and a list of materials before the inspector will grant a work permit for your job.

The National Electrical Code requires receptacles to be spaced no more than 12 ft. apart, but for convenience you can space them as close as 6 ft. apart. Also consider the placement of furniture in the finished room, and do not place receptacles or baseboard heaters where beds, desks, or couches will cover them.

Electric heating units are most effective if you position them on the outside walls, underneath the windows. Position the receptacles to the sides of the heating units, not above the heaters where high temperatures might damage electrical cords.

Room light fixtures should be centered in the room, while stairway lights must be positioned so each step is illuminated. All wall switches should be within easy reach of the room entrance. Include a smoke alarm if your room addition includes a sleeping area.

Installing a ceiling fan improves heating and cooling efficiency and is a good idea for any room addition. Position it in a central location, and make sure there is plenty of headroom beneath it. Also consider adding accessory wiring for telephone outlets, television jacks, or stereo speakers.

Tips for Planning Room Addition Circuits

A permanently wired smoke alarm (page 85) is required by local Building Codes for room additions that include sleeping areas. Plan to install the smoke alarm just outside the sleeping area, in a hallway or stairway. Battery-operated smoke detectors are not allowed in new room additions.

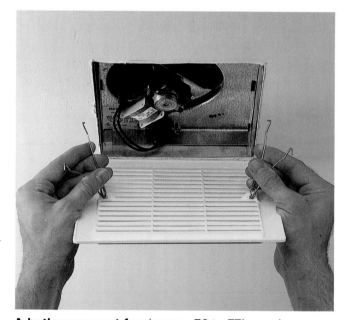

A bathroom vent fan (pages 76 to 77) may be required by your local Building Code, especially if your bathroom does not have a window. Vent fans are rated according to room size. Find the bathroom size in square feet by multiplying the length of the room times its width, and buy a vent fan rated for this size.

If your room addition includes a bathroom, it will have special wiring needs. All bathrooms require one or more GFCI receptacles, and most need a vent fan. An electric blower-heater will make your bathroom more comfortable.

Before drawing diagrams and applying for a work permit, calculate the electrical load (pages 14 to 17). Make sure your main service provides enough power for the new circuits.

Refer to pages 18 to 31 when drawing your wiring diagram. Using the completed diagram as a guide, create a detailed list of the materials you need. Bring the wiring diagram and the materials list to the inspector's office when you apply for the work permit. If the inspector suggests changes or improvements to your circuit design, follow his advice. His suggestions can save you time and money, and will ensure a safe, professional wiring installation.

A wiring plan for a room addition should show the location of all partition walls, doorways, and windows. Mark the location of all new and existing plumbing fixtures, water lines, drains, and vent pipes. Draw in any chimneys and duct work for central heating and air-conditioning systems. Make sure the plan is drawn to scale, because the size of the space will determine how you route the electrical cables and arrange the receptacles and fixtures.

Blower-heaters with built-in thermostats (pages 74, 86) work well in small areas like bathrooms, where quick heat is important. Some models can be wired for either 120 or 240 volts. A bathroom blower-heater should be placed well away from the sink and tub, at a comfortable height where the controls are easy to reach. In larger rooms, electric baseboard heaters controlled by a wall thermostat are more effective than blower-heaters.

Telephone and cable television wiring (pages 78 to 79) is easy to install at the same time you are installing electrical circuits. Position the accessory outlets in convenient locations, and keep the wiring at least 6" away from the electrical circuits to prevent static interference.

2: Install Boxes & Cables

For efficiency, install the electrical boxes for all new circuits before running any of the cables. After all the cables are installed, your project is ready for the rough-in inspection. Do not make the final connections until your work has passed rough-in inspection.

Boxes: See pages 36 to 41 for information on choosing and installing standard electrical boxes. In addition, your room addition may have recessed fixtures, like a blower-heater (photo, right) or vent fan (pages 76 to 77). These recessed fixtures have built-in wire connection boxes, and should be installed at the same time you are installing the standard electrical boxes. For a ceiling fan or other heavy ceiling fixture, install a metal box and brace bar (page opposite).

Cables: See pages 44 to 49 to install NM cable. In addition, you can install the necessary wiring for telephone outlets and cable television jacks (pages 78 to 79). This wiring is easy to install at the same time you are running electrical circuits, and is not subject to formal inspection.

How to Install a Blower-Heater

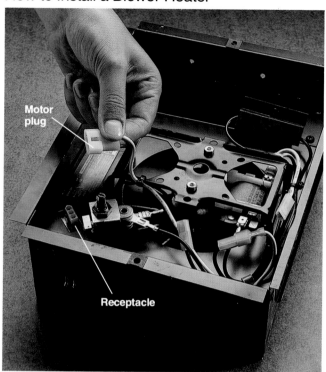

Motor plug

Receptacle

1 Disconnect the motor plug from the built-in receptacle that extends through the motor plate from the wire connection box.

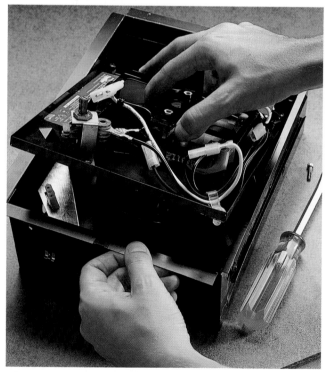

2 Take out the motor unit by removing the mounting screw and sliding the unit out of the frame.

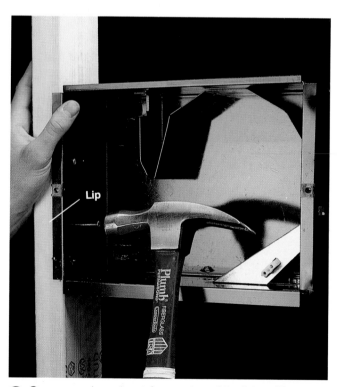

Lip

3 Open one knockout for each cable that will enter the wire connection box. Attach a cable clamp to each knockout. Position frame against a wall stud so the front lip will be flush with the finished wall surface. Attach the frame as directed by the manufacturer.

How to Install a Metal Box & Brace Bar for a Ceiling Fan

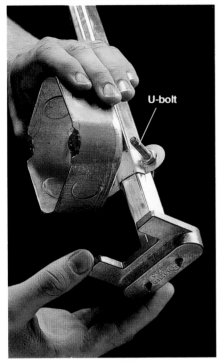

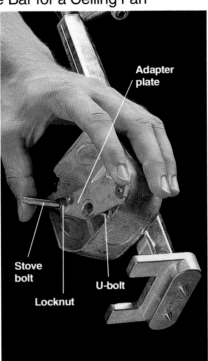

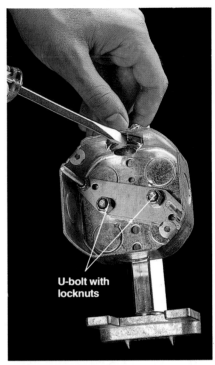

1 Attach a 1½"-deep metal light fixture box to the brace bar, using a U-bolt and two nuts.

2 Attach the included stove bolts to the adapter plate with locknuts. These bolts will support the fan. Insert the adapter plate into the box so ends of U-bolt fit through the holes on the adapter plate.

3 Secure the adapter plate by screwing two locknuts onto the U-bolt. Open one knockout for each cable that will enter the electrical box, and attach a cable clamp to each knockout.

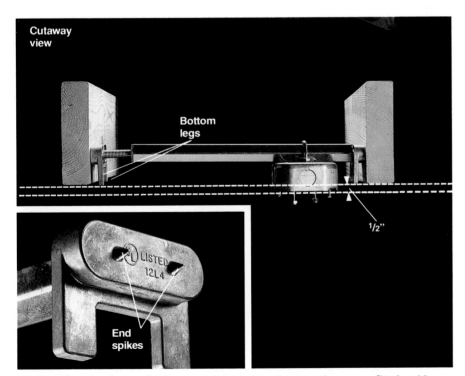

4 Position the brace between joists so the bottom legs are flush with the bottom of the joists. Rotate the bar by hand to force the end spikes into the joists. The face of the electrical box should be below the joists so the box will be flush with the finished ceiling surface.

5 Tighten the brace bar one rotation with a wrench to anchor the brace tightly against the joists.

Installing a Vent Fan

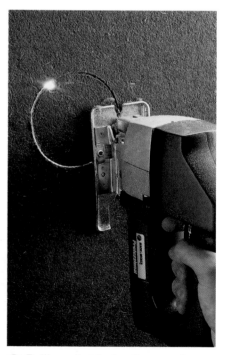

A vent fan helps prevent moisture damage to a bathroom by exhausting humid air to the outdoors. Vent fans are rated to match different room sizes. A vent fan can be controlled by a wall-mounted timer or single-pole switch. Some models have built-in light fixtures.

Position the vent fan in the center of the bathroom or over the stool area. In colder regions, Building Codes require that the vent hose be wrapped with insulation to prevent condensation of the moist air passing through the hose.

A vent fan has a built-in motor and blower that exhausts moisture-laden air from a bathroom to the outdoors through a plastic vent hose. A two-wire cable from a wall-mounted timer or single-pole switch is attached to the fan wire connection box with a cable clamp. A louvered coverplate mounted on the outside wall seals the vent against outdoor air when the motor is stopped.

How to Install a Vent Fan

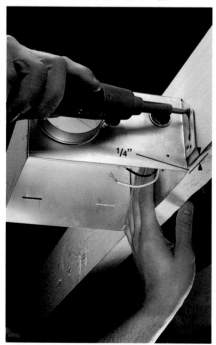

1 Disassemble the fan, following manufacturer's directions. Position the frame against a rafter so edge extends 1/4" below bottom edge of rafter to provide proper spacing for grill cover. Anchor frame with wallboard screws.

2 Choose the exit location for the vent. Temporarily remove any insulation, and draw the outline of the vent flange opening on the wall sheathing.

3 Drill a pilot hole, then make the cutout by sawing through the sheathing and siding with a jig saw. Keep the blade to the outside edge of the guideline.

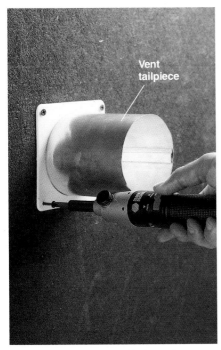

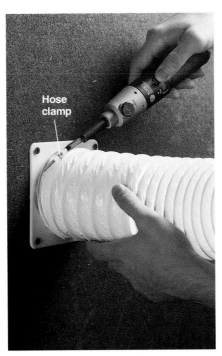

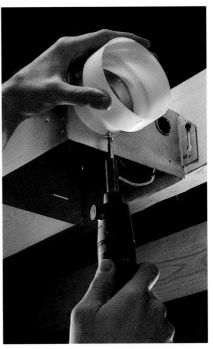

4 Insert the vent tailpiece into the cutout, and attach it to the wall by driving wallboard screws through the flange and into the sheathing.

5 Slide one end of vent hose over the tailpiece. Place one of the hose clamps around the end of the vent hose and tighten with a screwdriver. Replace insulation against sheathing.

6 Attach a hose adapter to the outlet on the fan frame by driving sheet-metal screws through the adapter and into the outlet flange. (NOTE: on some fans a hose adapter is not required.)

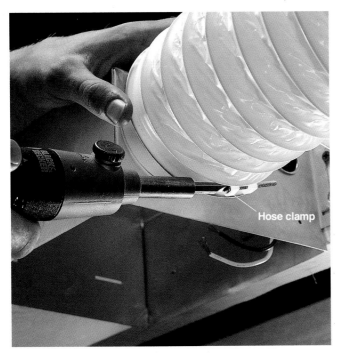

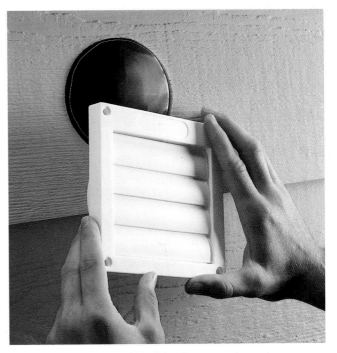

7 Slide the vent hose over the adapter. Place a hose clamp around the end of the hose and tighten it with a screwdriver. Your Building Code may require that you insulate the vent hose to prevent condensation problems.

8 On the outside wall of the house, place the louvered vent cover over the vent tailpiece, making sure the louvers are facing down. Attach the cover to the wall with galvanized screws. Apply a thick bead of caulk around the edge of the cover.

Arrange for the rough-in inspection before making the final connections.

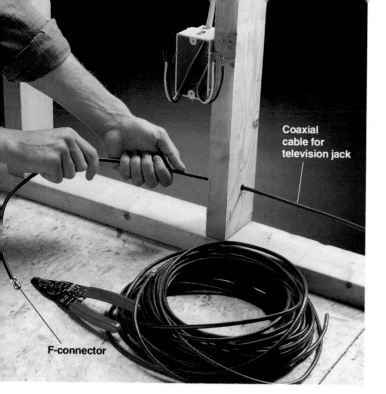

Coaxial cable for television jack

F-connector

Installing Telephone & Cable Television Wiring

Telephone outlets and television jacks are easy to install while you are wiring new electrical circuits. Install the accessory cables while framing members are exposed, then make the final connections after the walls are finished.

Telephone lines use four- or eight-wire cable, often called "bell wire," while television lines use a shielded coaxial cable with threaded end fittings called F-connectors. To splice into an existing cable television line, use a fitting called a signal splitter. Signal splitters are available with two, three, or four outlet nipples.

How to Install Coaxial Cable for a Television Jack

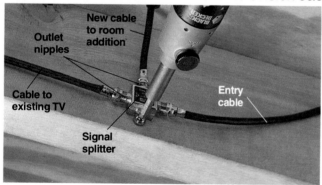

New cable to room addition

Outlet nipples

Cable to existing TV

Entry cable

Signal splitter

1 Install a signal splitter where the entry cable connects to indoor TV cables, usually in the basement or another utility area. Attach one end of new coaxial cable to an outlet nipple on the splitter. Anchor splitter to a framing member with wallboard screws.

2 Run the coaxial cable to the location of the new television jack. Keep coaxial cable at least 6" away from electrical wiring to avoid electrical interference. Mark the floor so the cable can be found easily after the walls are finished.

How to Connect a Television Jack

Mounting bracket

1 After walls are finished, make a cutout opening 1 1/2" wide and 3 3/4" high at the television jack location. Pull cable through the opening, and install two television jack mounting brackets in the cutout.

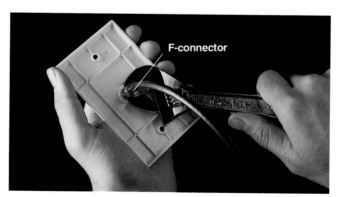

F-connector

2 Use a wrench to attach the cable F-connector to the back of the television jack. Attach the jack to the wall by screwing it onto the mounting brackets.

78

How to Install Cable for a Telephone Outlet

1 Locate a telephone junction in your basement or other utility area. Remove the junction cover. Use cable staples to anchor one end of the cable to a framing member near the junction, leaving 6" to 8" of excess cable.

2 Run the cable from the junction to the telephone outlet location. Keep the cable at least 6" away from circuit wiring to avoid electrical interference. Mark the floor so the cable can be located easily after the walls are finished.

How to Connect a Telephone Outlet

1 After walls are finished, cut a hole in the wallboard at phone outlet location, using a wallboard saw. Retrieve the cable, using a piece of stiff wire.

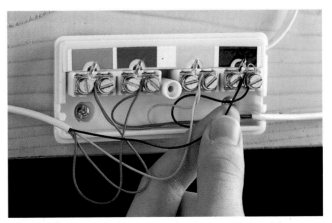

2 At each cable end, remove about 2" of outer sheathing. Remove about 3/4" of insulation from each wire, using a combination tool.

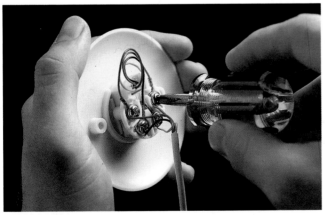

3 Connect wires to similarly colored wire leads in phone outlet. If there are extra wires, tape them to back of outlet. Put the telephone outlet over the wall cutout, and attach it to the wallboard.

4 At the telephone junction, connect the cable wires to the color-coded screw terminals. If there are extra wires, wrap them with tape and tuck them inside the junction. Reattach the junction cover.

3: Make Final Connections

Make the final connections for receptacles, switches, and fixtures only after the rough-in inspection is done and all walls and ceilings are finished. Use the circuit maps on pages 21 to 31 as a guide for making connections. The circuit maps are especially useful if your wiring configurations differ from those shown on the following pages. The last step is to hook up the new circuits at the breaker panel (pages 58 to 59).

After all connections are done, your work is ready for the final inspection. If you have worked carefully, the final inspection will take only a few minutes. The inspector may open one or two electrical boxes to check wire connections, and will check the circuit breaker hookups to make sure they are correct.

Materials You Will Need:

Pigtail wires, wire nuts, green & black tape.

Circuit #1

A 15-amp, 120-volt circuit serving the bathroom & closet.

- Timer & single-pole switch
- Vent fan
- Two light fixtures
- GFCI receptacle
- Single-pole switch
- 15-amp single-pole circuit breaker (see pages 58 to 59 for instructions on hooking up the circuit at the circuit breaker panel)

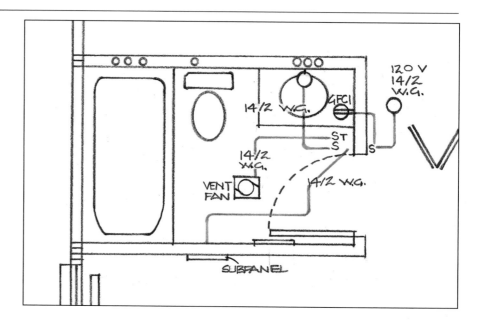

How to Connect the Timer & Single-pole Switch

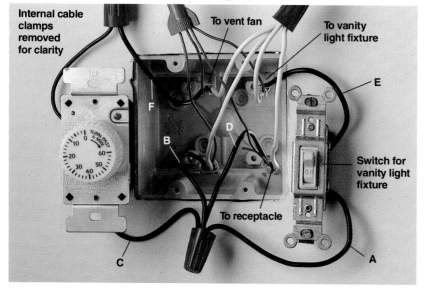

Internal cable clamps removed for clarity

To vent fan

To vanity light fixture

E

F

D

B

Switch for vanity light fixture

To receptacle

C

A

Attach a black pigtail wire (A) to one of the screw terminals on the switch. Use a wire nut to connect this pigtail to the black feed wire (B), to one of the black wire leads on the timer (C), and to the black wire carrying power to the bathroom receptacle (D). Connect the black wire leading to the vanity light fixture (E) to the remaining screw terminal on the switch. Connect the black wire running to the vent fan (F) to the remaining wire lead on the timer. Use wire nuts to join the white wires and the grounding wires. Tuck all wires into the box, then attach the switches, coverplate and timer dial. (See also circuit map 4, page 22, and circuit map 16, page 28.)

How to Connect the Vent Fan

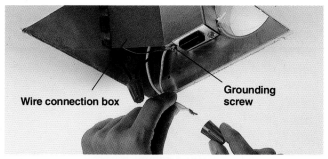

Wire connection box

Grounding screw

Mounting screw

In the wire connection box (top) connect black circuit wire to black wire lead on fan, using a wire nut. Connect white circuit wire to white wire lead. Connect grounding wire to the green grounding screw. **Insert the fan motor unit** (bottom) and attach mounting screws. Connect the fan motor plug to the built-in receptacle on the wire connection box. Attach the fan grill to the frame, using the mounting clips included with the fan kit (page 76).

How to Connect Light Fixtures

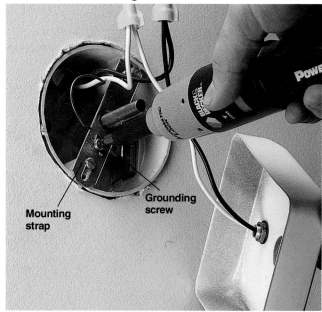

Mounting strap

Grounding screw

Attach a mounting strap with threaded nipple to the box, if required by the light fixture manufacturer. Connect the black circuit wire to the black wire lead on the light fixture, and connect the white circuit wire to the white wire lead. Connect the circuit grounding wire to the grounding screw on the mounting strap. Carefully tuck all wires into the electrical box, then position the fixture over the nipple and attach it with the mounting nut. (See also circuit map 4, page 22.)

How to Connect the Bathroom GFCI Receptacle

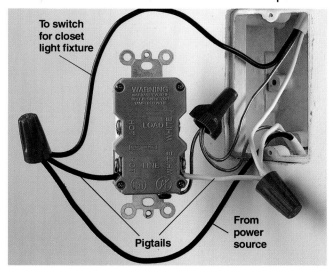

To switch for closet light fixture

Pigtails

From power source

Attach a black pigtail wire to brass screw terminal marked LINE. Join all black wires with a wire nut. Attach a white pigtail wire to the silver screw terminal marked LINE, then join all white wires with a wire nut. Attach a grounding pigtail to the green grounding screw, then join all grounding wires. Tuck all wires into the box, then attach the receptacle and the coverplate. (See also circuit map 2, page 21.)

How to Connect the Single-pole Switch

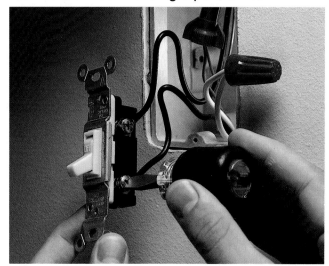

Attach the black circuit wires to the brass screw terminals on the switch. Use wire nuts to join the white neutral wires together and the bare copper grounding wires together. Tuck all wires into the box, then attach the switch and the coverplate. (See also circuit map 4, page 22.)

Circuit #2:

A 15-amp, 120-volt isolated-ground circuit for a home computer in the office area.

- 15-amp isolated-ground receptacle
- 15-amp single-pole circuit breaker (see pages 58 to 59 for instructions on hooking up the circuit at the circuit breaker panel)

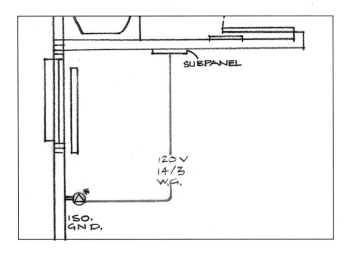

How to Connect the Computer Receptacle

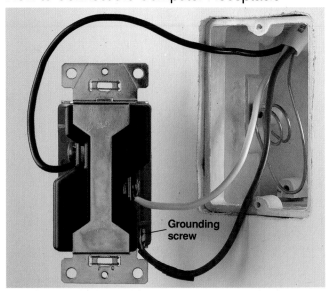

Grounding screw

Tag the red wire with green tape to identify it as a grounding wire. Attach this wire to the grounding screw terminal on the isolated-ground receptacle. Connect the black wire to the brass screw terminal, and the white wire to the silver screw. Push the bare copper wire to the back of the box. Carefully tuck all wires into the box, then attach the receptacle and coverplate. (See also circuit map 15, page 28.)

Circuit #3:

A 20-amp, 240-volt air-conditioner circuit.

- 20-amp, 240-volt receptacle (singleplex or duplex style)
- 20-amp double-pole circuit breaker (see pages 58 to 59 for instructions on hooking up the circuit at the circuit breaker panel)

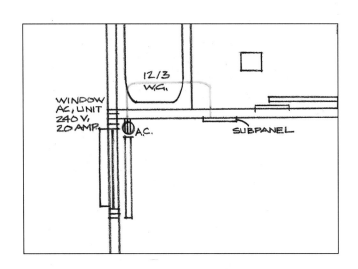

How to Connect the 240-volt Receptacle

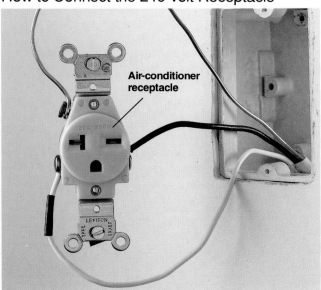

Air-conditioner receptacle

Connect the black circuit wire to a brass screw terminal on the air-conditioner receptacle, and connect the white circuit wire to the screw on the opposite side. Tag white wire with black tape to identify it as a hot wire. Connect grounding wire to green grounding screw on the receptacle. Tuck in wires, then attach receptacle and coverplate. (See also circuit map 12, page 26.) A 240-volt receptacle is available in either singleplex (shown above) or duplex style.

■ Circuit #4:

A 15-amp, 120-volt basic lighting/receptacle circuit serving the office and bedroom areas.

- Single-pole switch for split receptacle, three-way switch for stairway light fixture
- Speed-control and dimmer switches for ceiling fan
- Switched duplex receptacle
- 15-amp, 120-volt receptacles
- Ceiling fan with light fixture
- Smoke detector
- Stairway light fixture
- 15-amp single-pole circuit breaker (see pages 58 to 59)

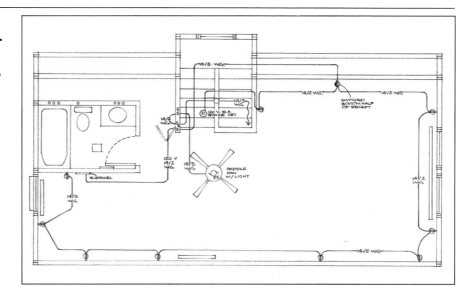

How to Connect Switches for Receptacle & Stairway Light

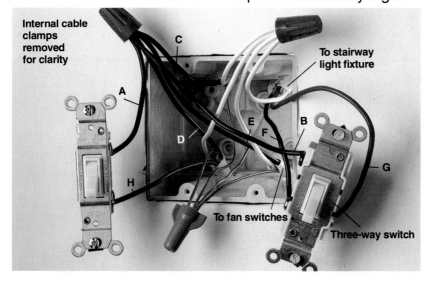

Internal cable clamps removed for clarity

To stairway light fixture

To fan switches

Three-way switch

Attach a black pigtail wire (A) to one of the screws on the single-pole switch and another black pigtail (B) to common screw on three-way switch. Use a wire nut to connect pigtail wires to black feed wire (C), to black wire running to unswitched receptacles (D), and to the black wire running to fan switches (E). Connect remaining wires running to light fixture (F, G) to traveler screws on three-way switch. Connect red wire running to switched receptacle (H) to remaining screw on single-pole switch. Use wire nuts to join white wires and grounding wires. Tuck all wires into box, then attach switches and coverplate. (See also circuit map 7, page 24, and map 17, page 29.)

How to Connect the Ceiling Fan Switches

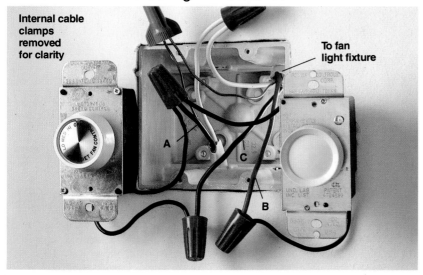

Internal cable clamps removed for clarity

To fan light fixture

Connect the black feed wire (A) to one of the black wire leads on each switch, using a wire nut. Connect the red circuit wire (B) running to the fan light fixture to the remaining wire lead on the dimmer switch. Connect the black circuit wire (C) running to the fan motor to the remaining wire lead on the speed-control switch. Use wire nuts to join the white wires and the grounding wires. Tuck all wires into the box, then attach the switches, coverplate, and switch dials. (See also circuit map 21, page 31.)

How to Connect a Switched Receptacle

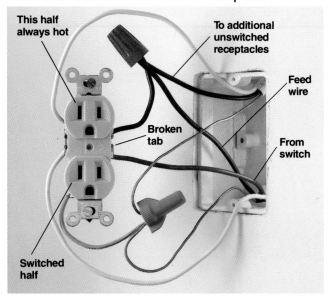

Break the connecting tab between the brass screw terminals on the receptacle, using needlenose pliers. Attach the red wire to the bottom brass screw. Connect a black pigtail wire to the other brass screw, then connect all black wires with a wire nut. Connect white wires to silver screws. Attach a grounding pigtail to the green grounding screw, then join all the grounding wires, using a wire nut. Tuck the wires into the box, then attach the receptacle and coverplate. (See also circuit map 7, page 24.)

How to Connect Receptacles

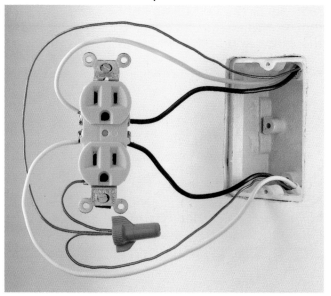

Connect the black circuit wires to the brass screw terminals on the receptacle, and the white wires to the silver terminals. Attach a grounding pigtail to the green grounding screw on the receptacle, then join all grounding wires with a wire nut. Tuck the wires into the box, then attach the receptacle and coverplate. (See also circuit map 1, page 21.)

How to Connect a Ceiling Fan/Light Fixture

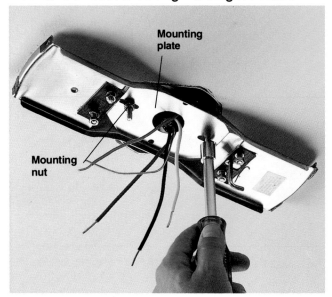

1 Place the ceiling fan mounting plate over the stove bolts extending through the electrical box. Pull the circuit wires through the hole in the center of the mounting plate. Attach the mounting nuts and tighten them with a nut driver.

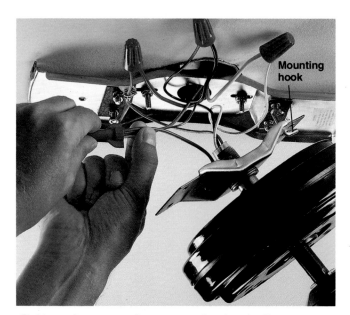

2 Hang fan motor from mounting hook. Connect black circuit wire to black wire lead from fan, using a wire nut. Connect red circuit wire from dimmer to blue wire lead from light fixture, white circuit wire to white lead, and grounding wires to green lead. Complete assembly of fan and light fixture, following manufacturer's directions. (See also circuit map 21, page 30.)

How to Connect a Smoke Alarm

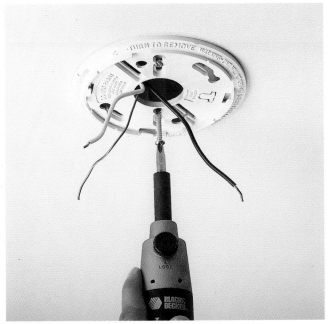

1 Attach the smoke alarm mounting plate to the electrical box, using the mounting screws provided with the smoke alarm kit.

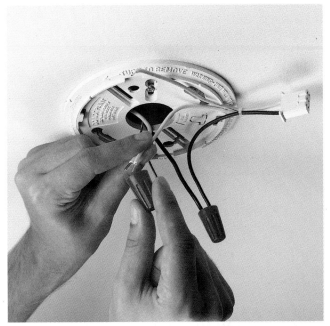

2 Use wire nuts to connect the black circuit wire to the black wire lead on the smoke alarm, and the white circuit wire to the white wire lead.

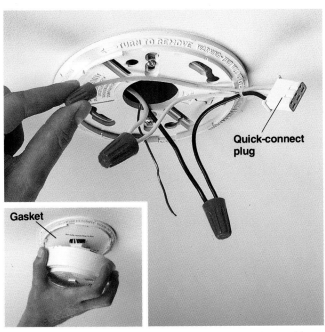

Quick-connect plug

Gasket

3 Screw a wire nut onto the end of the yellow wire, if present. (This wire is used only if two or more alarms are wired in series.) Tuck all wires into the box Place the cardboard gasket over the mounting plate. Attach the quick-connect plug to the smoke alarm. Attach the alarm to the mounting plate, twisting it clockwise until it locks into place (inset).

How to Connect a Stairway Light Fixture

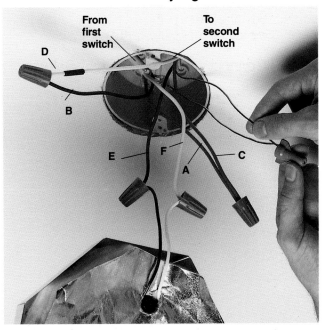

From first switch

To second switch

D

B

E F C

A

Connect the traveler wires entering the box from the first three-way switch (red wire [A] and black wire [B]) to the traveler wires running to the second three-way switch (red wire [C] and white wire tagged with black tape [D]). Connect the common wire running to the second switch (E) to the black lead on the light fixture. Connect the white wire from the first switch (F) to the white fixture lead. Join the grounding wires. Tuck wires into box and attach the light fixture. (See also circuit map 17, page 29.)

■ Circuit #5:

A 20-amp, 240-volt circuit serving the bathroom blower-heater, and three baseboard heaters controlled by a wall thermostat.

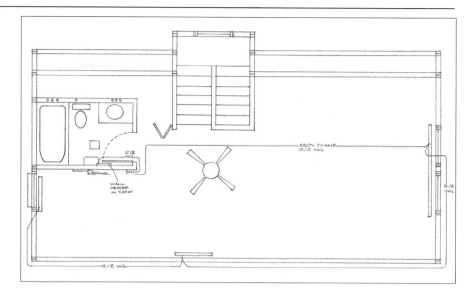

- 240-volt blower-heater
- 240-volt thermostat
- 240-volt baseboard heaters
- 20-amp double-pole circuit breaker (see pages 58 to 59 for instructions on hooking up the circuit at the circuit) breaker panel)

How to Connect a 240-volt Blower-Heater

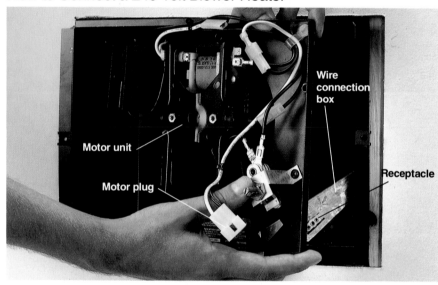

Wire connection box

Motor unit

Motor plug

Receptacle

Blower-heaters: In the heater's wire connection box, connect one of the wire leads to the white circuit wires, and the other wire lead to the black circuit wires, using same method as for baseboard heaters (page opposite). Insert the motor unit, and attach the motor plug to the built-in receptacle. Attach the coverplate and thermostat knob. NOTE: Some types of blower-heaters can be wired for either 120 volts or 240 volts. If you have this type, make sure the internal plug connections are configured for 240 volts.

How to Connect a 240-volt Thermostat

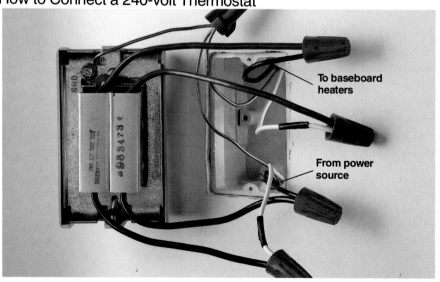

To baseboard heaters

From power source

Connect the red wire leads on the thermostat to the circuit wires entering the box from the power source, using wire nuts. Connect black wire leads to circuit wires leading to the baseboard heaters. Tag the white wires with black tape to indicate they are hot. Attach a grounding pigtail to the grounding screw on the thermostat, then connect all grounding wires. Tuck the wires into the box, then attach the thermostat and coverplate. (See also circuit map 13, page 27.) Follow manufacturer's directions: the color coding for thermostats may vary.

How to Connect 240-volt Baseboard Heaters

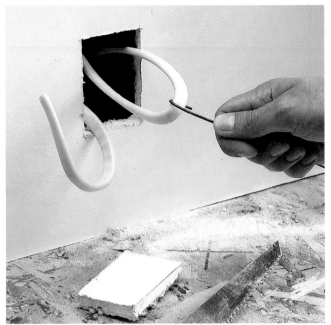

1 At the cable location, cut a small hole in the wallboard, 3" to 4" above the floor, using a wallboard saw. Pull the cables through the hole, using a piece of stiff wire with a hook on the end. Middle-of-run heaters will have 2 cables, while end-of-run heaters have only 1 cable.

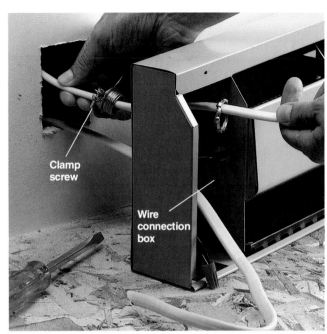

2 Remove the cover on the wire connection box. Open a knockout for each cable that will enter the box, then feed the cables through the cable clamps and into the wire connection box. Attach the clamps to the wire connection box, and tighten the clamp screws until the cables are gripped firmly.

3 Anchor heater against wall, about 1" off floor, by driving flat-head screws through back of housing and into studs. Strip away cable sheathing so at least 1/4" of sheathing extends into the heater. Strip 3/4" of insulation from each wire, using a combination tool.

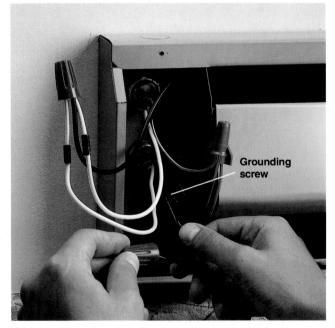

4 Use wire nuts to connect the white circuit wires to one of the wire leads on the heater. Tag white wires with black tape to indicate they are hot. Connect the black circuit wires to the other wire lead. Connect a grounding pigtail to the green grounding screw in the box, then join all grounding wires with a wire nut. Reattach cover. (See also circuit map 13, page 27.)

Make hookups at circuit breaker panel (page 58) and arrange for final inspection.

Choose the Fixtures You Need

A: Range receptacle (circuit #3) supplies power for a range/oven combination appliance on a dedicated circuit. See page 102.

B: 20-amp receptacles (circuits #1 & #2) supply power for small appliances. See page 100.

C: Under-cabinet task lights (circuit #7) provide fluorescent light for countertop work areas. See page 105.

D: Microwave receptacle (circuit #4) supplies power for a microwave on a dedicated circuit. See page 102.

E: GFCI receptacles (circuits #1 & #2) provide protection against shock. See page 101.

Wiring a Remodeled Kitchen

The kitchen is the greatest power user in your home. Adding new circuits during a kitchen remodeling project will make your kitchen better serve your needs. This section shows how to install new circuit wiring when remodeling. You learn how to plan for the many power requirements of the modern kitchen, and techniques for doing the work before the walls and ceiling are finished.

This section takes you through all phases of the project: evaluating your existing service, planning the new work and getting a permit, installing the circuits, and having your work inspected.

You learn how to install circuits and fixtures for recessed lights, under-cabinet task lights, and a ceiling light controlled by three-way switches. You also learn how to install circuits and receptacles for a range, microwave, dishwasher, and food disposer. Methods for installing two small-appliance circuits are also shown.

While your kitchen remodeling project will differ from this one, the methods and concepts shown apply to any kitchen wiring project containing any combination of circuits.

The next two pages show the circuits in place with the walls and ceiling removed.

Photo courtesy of Kitchens by Krengel, Inc.

F: Ceiling fixture (circuit #7) provides general lighting for the entire kitchen. It is controlled by two three-way switches located by the doors to the room. See page 104.

G: Food disposer receptacle (circuit #5) is controlled by a switch near the sink and supplies power to the disposer located in the sink cabinet. See page 103.

H: Dishwasher receptacle (circuit #6) supplies power for the dishwasher on a dedicated circuit. See page 103.

I: Recessed fixtures (circuit #7) controlled by switches near the sink provide additional lighting for work areas at sink, range, and countertop. See page 105.

14/2 cable

12/3 cable

12/2 cable

6/3 cable

14/2 cable

Learn How to Install These Circuits

#1 & #2: Small-appliance circuits. Two 20-amp, 120-volt circuits supply power to countertop and eating areas for small appliances. All general-use receptacles must be on these circuits. One 12/3 cable, fed by a 20-amp double-pole breaker, wires both circuits. These circuits share one electrical box with the disposer circuit (#5), and another with the basic lighting circuit (#7).

#3: Range circuit. A 50-amp, 120/240-volt dedicated circuit supplies power to the range/oven appliance. It is wired with 6/3 cable.

#4: Microwave circuit. A dedicated 20-amp, 120-volt circuit supplies power to the microwave. It is wired with 12/2 cable. Microwaves that use less than 300 watts can be installed on a 15-amp circuit, or plugged into the small-appliance circuits.

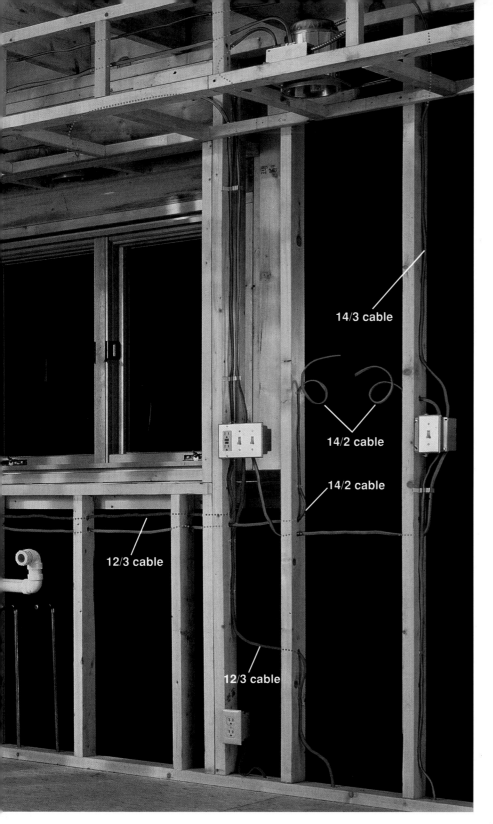

14/3 cable

14/2 cable

14/2 cable

12/3 cable

12/3 cable

Wiring a Remodeled Kitchen:
Construction View

The kitchen remodeling wiring project shown on the following pages includes the installation of seven new circuits. Four of these are dedicated circuits: a 50-amp circuit supplying the range, a 20-amp circuit powering the microwave, and two 15-amp circuits supplying the dishwasher and food disposer. In addition, two 20-amp circuits for small appliances supply power to all receptacles above the countertops and in the eating area. Finally, a 15-amp basic lighting circuit controls the ceiling fixture, all of the recessed fixtures, and the under-cabinet task lights.

All rough construction and plumbing work should be finished and inspected before beginning the electrical work. Divide the project into steps and complete each step before beginning the next.

Three Steps for Wiring a Remodeled Kitchen:

1. Plan the circuits (pages 94 to 95).
2. Install boxes and cables (pages 96 to 99).
3. Make final connections (pages 100 to 105).

Tools You Will Need:
Marker, tape measure, calculator, masking tape, screwdriver, hammer, power drill with 5/8" spade bit, cable ripper, combination tool, needlenose pliers, fish tape.

■ **#5: Food disposer circuit.** A dedicated 15-amp, 120-volt circuit supplies power to the disposer. It is wired with 14/2 cable. Some local Codes allow the disposer to be on the same circuit as the dishwasher.

■ **#6: Dishwasher circuit.** A dedicated 15-amp, 120-volt circuit supplies power to the dishwasher. It is wired with 14/2 cable. Some local Codes allow the dishwasher to be on the same circuit as the disposer.

■ **#7: Basic lighting circuit.** A 15-amp, 120-volt circuit powers the ceiling fixture, recessed fixtures, and under-cabinet task lights. 14/2 and 14/3 cables connect the fixtures and switches in the circuit. Each task light has a self-contained switch.

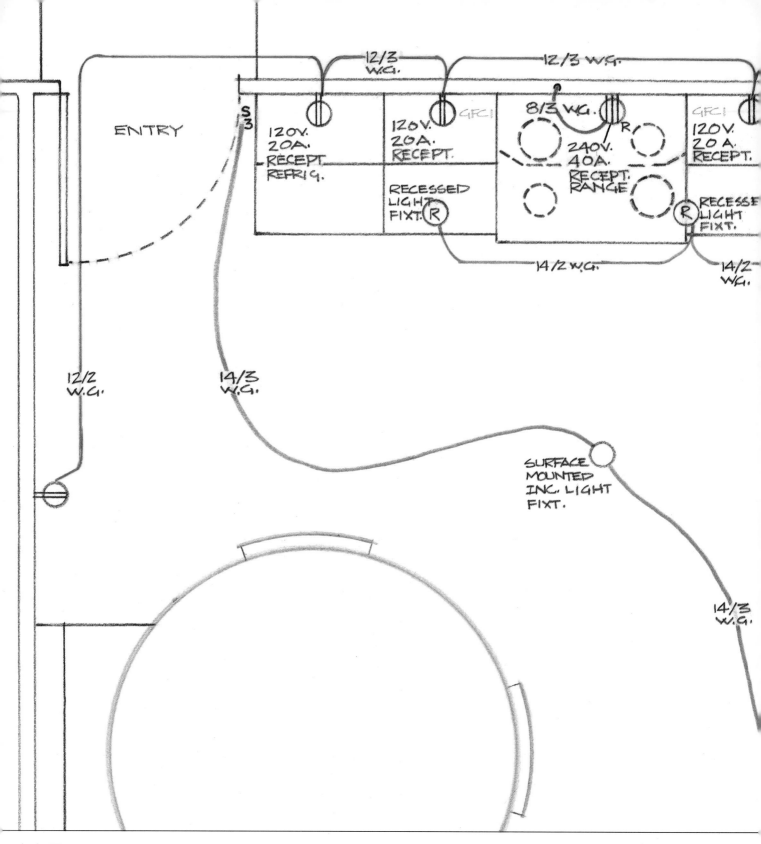

ENTRY

12/3 W.G.

12/3 W.G.

S 3

120V. 20A. RECEPT. REFRIG.

120V. 20A. RECEPT.

GFCI

8/3 W.G.

R

240V. 40A. RECEPT. RANGE

GFCI

120V. 20A. RECEPT.

RECESSED LIGHT FIXT. R

RECESSED LIGHT FIXT. R

14/2 W.G.

14/2 W.G.

12/2 W.G.

14/3 W.G.

SURFACE MOUNTED INC. LIGHT FIXT.

14/3 W.G.

Circuits #1 & #2: Two 20-amp, 120-volt small-appliance circuits wired with one cable. All general-use receptacles must be on these circuits and they must be GFCI units. Includes: 7 GFCI receptacles rated for 20 amps, 5 electrical boxes that are 4" × 4", and 12/3 cable. One GFCI shares a double-gang box with circuit #5, and another GFCI shares a triple-gang box with circuit #7.

Circuit #3: A 50-amp, 120/240-volt dedicated circuit for the range. Includes: a 4" × 4" box; a 120/240-volt, 50-amp range receptacle; and 6/3 NM cable.

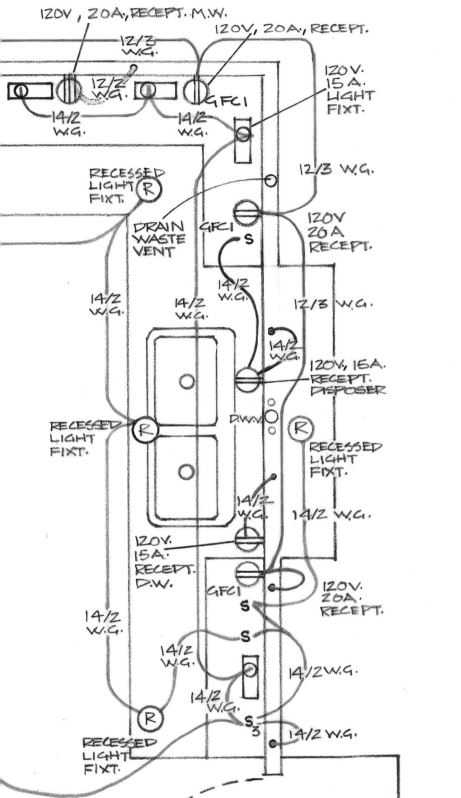

The following labels appear within the diagram:

- 120V, 20A, RECEPT. M.W.
- 12/3 W.G.
- 12/2 W.G.
- 120V, 20A, RECEPT.
- 120V, 15A, LIGHT FIXT.
- 14/2 W.G.
- 14/2 W.G.
- GFCI
- RECESSED LIGHT FIXT. (R)
- 12/3 W.G.
- DRAIN WASTE VENT
- GFCI
- S
- 120V, 20A, RECEPT.
- 14/2 W.G.
- 14/2 W.G.
- 14/2 W.G.
- 12/3 W.G.
- 14/2 W.G.
- 120V, 15A, RECEPT. DISPOSER
- RECESSED LIGHT FIXT. (R)
- D.W.V.
- RECESSED LIGHT FIXT. (R)
- 14/2 W.G.
- 14/2 W.G.
- 120V, 15A, RECEPT. D.W.
- GFCI
- 120V, 20A, RECEPT.
- 14/2 W.G.
- S
- S
- 14/2 W.G.
- 14/2 W.G.
- 14/2 W.G.
- 14/2 W.G.
- S3
- 14/2 W.G.
- RECESSED LIGHT FIXT. (R)

Wiring a Remodeled Kitchen: Diagram View

This diagram view shows the layout of seven circuits and the location of the switches, receptacles, lights, and other fixtures in the remodeled kitchen featured in this section. The size and number of circuits, and the specific features included are based on the needs of this 170-sq. ft. space. No two remodeled kitchens are exactly alike, so create your own wiring diagram to guide you through your wiring project.

Note:
See pages 18 to 19 for a key to the common electrical symbols used in this diagram, and to learn how to draw your own wiring diagrams.

Circuit #7: A 15-amp, 120-volt basic lighting circuit serving all of the lighting needs in the kitchen. Includes: 2 single-pole switches, 2 three-way switches, single-gang box, 4" × 4" box, triple-gang box (shared with one of the GFCI receptacles from the small-appliance circuits), plastic light fixture box with brace, ceiling light fixture, 4 fluorescent under-cabinet light fixtures, 6 recessed light fixtures, 14/2 and 14/3 cable.

Circuit #6: A 15-amp, 120-volt dedicated circuit for the dishwasher. Includes: a 15-amp duplex receptacle, one single-gang box, and 14/2 cable.

Circuit #4: A 20-amp, 120-volt dedicated circuit for the microwave. Includes: a 20-amp duplex receptacle, a single-gang box, and 12/2 NM cable.

Circuit #5: A 15-amp, 120-volt dedicated circuit for the food disposer. Includes: a 15-amp duplex receptacle, a single-pole switch (installed in a double-gang box with a GFCI receptacle from the small-appliance circuits), one single-gang box, and 14/2 cable.

4 ft. maximum

Code requires receptacles above countertops to be no more than 4 ft. apart. Put receptacles closer together in areas where many appliances will be used. Any section of countertop that is wider than 12" must have a receptacle located above it. (Countertop spaces separated by items such as range tops, sinks, and refrigerators are considered separate sections.) All accessible receptacles in kitchens (and bathrooms) must be a GFCI. On walls without countertops, receptacles should be no more than 12 ft. apart.

Wiring a Remodeled Kitchen

1: Plan the Circuits

A kitchen generally uses the most power in the home because it contains many light fixtures and appliances. Where these items are located depends upon your needs. Make sure plenty of light and enough receptacles will be in the main work areas of your kitchen. Try to anticipate future needs: for example, install a range receptacle when remodeling, even if you currently have a gas range. It is difficult and expensive to make changes later. See pages 6 to 19 for more information on planning circuits.

Contact your local Building and Electrical Code offices before you begin planning. They may have requirements that differ from the National Electrical Code. Remember that the Code contains minimum requirements primarily concerning safety, not convenience or need. Work with the inspectors to create a safe plan that also meets your needs.

To help locate receptacles, plan carefully where cabinets and appliances will be in the finished project. Appliances installed within cabinets, such as microwaves or food disposers, must have their receptacles positioned according to manufacturer's instructions. Put at least one receptacle at table height in the dining areas for convenience in operating a small appliance.

The ceiling fixture should be centered in the kitchen ceiling. Or, if your kitchen contains a dining area or breakfast nook, you may want to center the light fixture over the table. Locate recessed light fixtures and under-cabinet task lights where they will best illuminate main work areas.

Before drawing diagrams and applying for a permit, evaluate your existing service and make sure it provides enough power to supply the new circuits you are planning to add (pages 14 to 17). If it will not, contact a licensed electrician to upgrade your service before beginning your work. See pages 18 to 31 for more information on drawing wiring plans.

Bring the wiring plan and materials list to the inspector's office when applying for the permit. If the inspector suggests improvements to your plan, such as using switches with grounding screws, follow his advice. He can save you time and money.

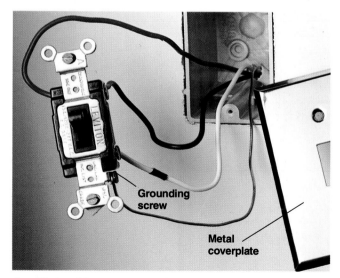

Grounding screw

Metal coverplate

A switch with a grounding screw may be required by inspectors in kitchens and baths. Code requires them when metal coverplates are used with plastic boxes.

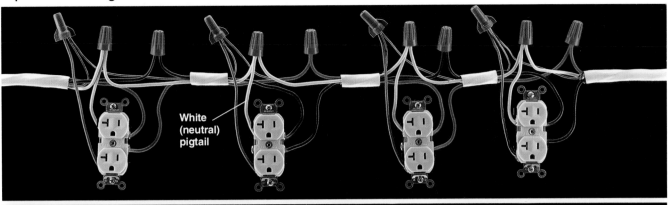

White (neutral) pigtail

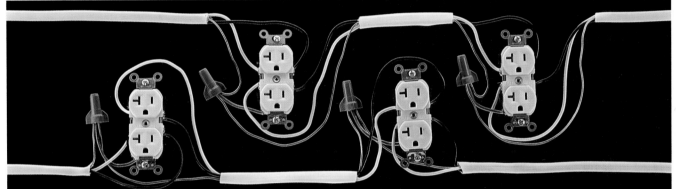

Two 20-amp small-appliance circuits can be wired with one 12/3 cable supplying power to both circuits (top), rather than using separate 12/2 cables for each circuit (bottom), to save time and money. Because these circuits must be GFCI protected, either place a GFCI receptacle first in each circuit (the remaining 20-amp duplex units are connected through the LOAD terminals on the GFCI) or use a GFCI receptacle at each location. In 12/3 cable, the black wire supplies power to one circuit for alternate receptacles (the first, third, etc.), the red wire supplies power for the second circuit to the remaining receptacles. The white wire is the neutral for both circuits (see circuit map 10, page 25). For safety, it must be attached with a pigtail to each receptacle, instead of being connected directly to the terminal. These circuits must contain all general-use receptacles in the kitchen, pantry, breakfast area or dining room. No lighting outlets or receptacles from any other rooms can be connected to them.

Work areas at sink and range should be well lighted for convenience and safety. Install switch-controlled lights over these areas.

Ranges require a dedicated 40- or 50-amp 120/240-volt circuit (or two circuits for separate oven and countertop units). Even if you do not have an electric range, it is a good idea to install tne circuit when remodeling.

Dishwashers and food disposers require dedicated 15-amp, 120-volt circuits in most local Codes. Some inspectors will allow these appliances to share one circuit.

Heights of electrical boxes in a kitchen vary depending upon their use. In the kitchen project shown here the centers of the boxes above the countertop are 45" above the floor, in the center of 18" backsplashes that extend from the countertop to the cabinets. All boxes for wall switches also are installed at this height.

The center of the box for the microwave receptacle is 72" off the floor, where it will fit between the cabinets. The centers of the boxes for the range and food disposer receptacles are 12" off the floor, but the center of the box for the dishwasher receptacle is 6" off the floor, next to the space the appliance will occupy.

Wiring a Remodeled Kitchen

2: Install Boxes & Cables

After the inspector issues you a work permit, you can begin installing electrical boxes for switches, receptacles, and fixtures. Install all boxes and frames for recessed fixtures such as vent fans and recessed lights before cutting and installing any cable. However, some surface-mounted fixtures, such as under-cabinet task lights, have self-contained wire connection boxes. These fixtures are installed after the walls are finished and the cabinets are in place.

First determine locations for the boxes above the countertops (page opposite). After establishing the height for these boxes, install all of the other visible wall boxes at this height. Boxes that will be behind appliances or inside cabinets should be located according to appliance manufacturer's

instructions. For example, the receptacle for the dishwasher cannot be installed directly behind the appliance; it is often located in the sink cabinet for easy access.

Always use the largest electrical boxes that are practical for your installation. Using large boxes ensures that you will meet Code regulations concerning box volume, and simplifies making the connections. See pages 36 to 41 for more information on choosing and installing standard electrical boxes.

After all the boxes and recessed fixtures are installed, you are ready to measure and cut the cables. First install the feeder cables that run from the circuit breaker panel to the first electrical box in each circuit. Then cut and install the remaining cables to complete the circuits. See pages 44 to 49 for information on installing NM cable.

Tips for Installing Boxes & Cables

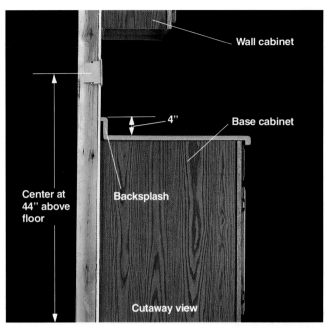

Use masking tape to outline the location of all cabinets, large appliances, and other openings. The outlines help you position the electrical boxes accurately. Remember to allow for moldings and other trim.

Standard backsplash height is 4"; the center of a box installed above this should be 44" above the floor. If the backsplash is more than 4" high, or the distance between the countertop and the bottom of the cabinet is less than 18", center the box in the space between the countertop and the bottom of the wall cabinet.

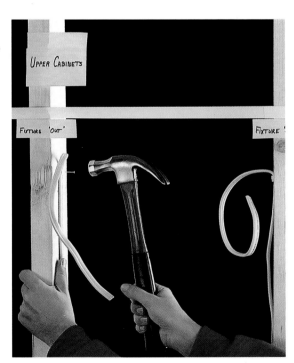

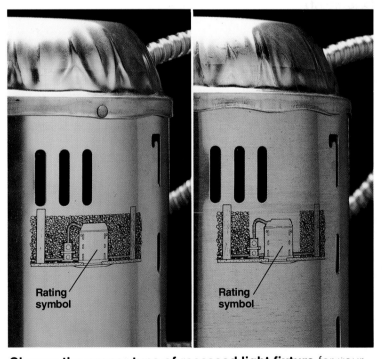

Install cables for an under-cabinet light at positions that will line up with the knockouts on the fixture box (which is installed after the walls and cabinets are in place). Cables will be retrieved through ⁵/8" drilled holes (page 105), so it is important to position the cables accurately.

Choose the proper type of recessed light fixture for your project. There are two types of fixtures: those rated for installation within insulation (left), and those which must be kept at least 3" from insulation (right). Self-contained thermal switches shut off power if the unit gets too hot for its rating. A recessed light fixture must be installed at least ¹/2" from combustible materials.

How to Mount a Recessed Light Fixture

1 Extend the mounting bars on the recessed fixture to reach the framing members. Adjust the position of the light unit on the mounting bars to locate it properly. Align the bottom edges of the mounting bars with the bottom face of the framing members.

2 Nail or screw the mounting bars to the framing members.

3 Remove the wire connection box cover and open one knockout for each cable entering the box.

4 Install a cable clamp for each open knockout, and tighten locknut, using a screwdriver to drive the lugs.

How to Install the Feeder Cable

1 Drill access holes through the sill plate where the feeder cables will enter from the circuit breaker panel. Choose spots that offer easy access to the circuit breaker panel as well as to the first electrical box on the circuit.

2 Drill ⁵/₈" holes through framing members to allow cables to pass from the circuit breaker panel to access holes. Front edge of hole should be at least 1¹/₄" from front edge of framing member.

3 For each circuit, measure and cut enough cable to run from circuit breaker panel, through access hole into the kitchen, to the first electrical box in the circuit. Add at least 2 ft. for the panel and 1 ft. for the box.

4 Anchor the cable with a cable staple within 12" of the panel. Extend cable through and along joists to access hole into kitchen, stapling every 4 ft. where necessary. Keep cable at least 1¹/₄" from front edge of framing members. Thread cable through access hole into kitchen, and on to the first box in the circuit. Continue circuit to rest of boxes (pages 44 to 47).

Arrange for the rough-in inspection before making the final connections.

3: Make Final Connections

Make the final connections for switches, receptacles, and fixtures after the rough-in inspection. First make final connections on recessed fixtures (it is easier to do this before wallboard is installed). Then finish the work on walls and ceiling, install the cabinets, and make the rest of the final connections. Use the photos on the following pages and the circuit maps on pages 20 to 31 as a guide

for making the final connections. The last step is to connect the circuits at the breaker panel (pages 58 to 59). After all connections are made, your work is ready for the final inspection.

Materials You Will Need:

Pigtail wires, wire nuts, black tape.

■ Circuits #1 & #2

Two 20-amp, 120-volt small-appliance circuits.

• 7 GFCI receptacles
• 20-amp double-pole circuit breaker (see pages 58 to 59 for instructions on making final connections at the circuit breaker panel)

Note: In this project, two of the GFCI receptacles are installed in boxes that also contain switches from other circuits (page opposite).

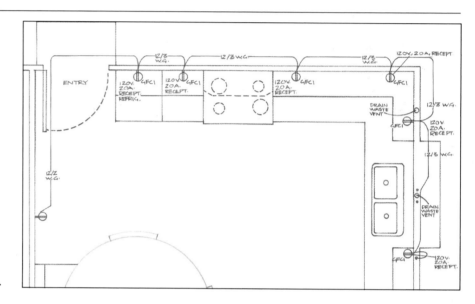

How to Connect Small-appliance Receptacles (that alternate on two 20-amp circuits in one 12/3 cable)

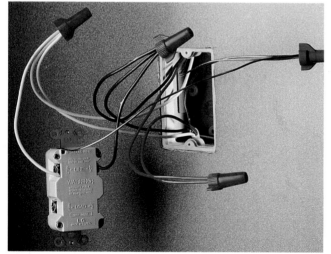

1 At alternate receptacles in the cable run (first, third, etc.), attach a black pigtail to brass screw terminal marked LINE on the receptacle and to black wire from both cables. Connect a white pigtail to a silver screw (LINE) and to both white wires. Connect a grounding pigtail to the grounding screw and to both grounding wires. Connect both red wires together. Tuck wires into box, then attach the receptacle and coverplate. (See circuit map 10, page 25.)

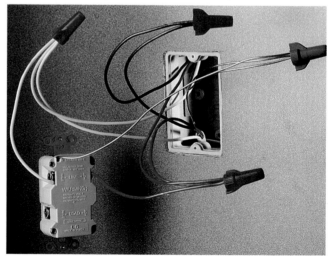

2 At remaining receptacles in the run, attach a red pigtail to a brass screw terminal (LINE) and to red wires from the cables. Attach a white pigtail to a silver screw terminal (LINE) and to both white wires. Connect a grounding pigtail to the grounding screw and to both grounding wires. Connect both black wires together. Tuck wires into box, attach receptacle and coverplate. (See page 95 for optional method of GFCI protection.)

How to Install a GFCI & a Disposer Switch

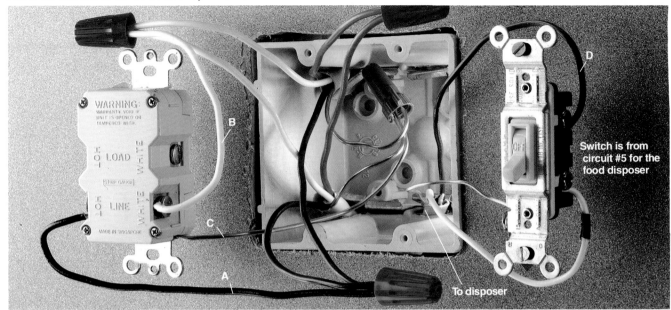

Connect black pigtail (A) to GFCI brass terminal marked LINE, and to black wires from three-wire cables. Attach white pigtail (B) to silver terminal marked LINE, and to white wires from three-wire cables. Attach grounding pigtail (C) to GFCI grounding screw and to grounding wires from three-wire cables. Connect both red wires to-

gether. (See circuit map 11, page 26.) Connect black wire from two-wire cable (D) to one switch terminal. Attach white wire to other terminal and tag it black indicating it is hot. Attach grounding wire to switch grounding screw. (See circuit map 5, page 23.) Tuck wires into box, attach switch, receptacle, and coverplate.

How to Install a GFCI & Two Switches for Recessed Lights

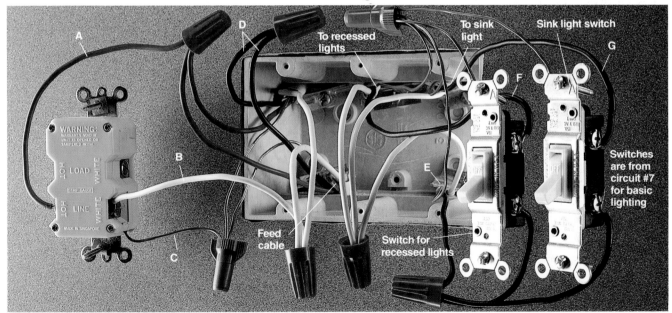

Connect red pigtail (A) to GFCI brass terminal labeled LINE, and to red wires from three-wire cables. Connect white pigtail (B) to silver LINE terminal, and to white wires from three-wire cables. Attach grounding pigtail (C) to grounding screw, and to grounding wires from three-wire cables. Connect black wires from three-wire cables (D) together. (See circuit map 11, page 26.) Attach a black pigtail to one screw on each switch and to black wire from two-wire feed cable (E).

Connect black wire (F) from the two-wire cable leading to recessed lights to remaining screw on the switch for the recessed lights. Connect black wire (G) from two-wire cable leading to sink light to remaining screw on sink light switch. Connect white wires from all two-wire cables together. Connect pigtails to switch grounding screws, and to all grounding wires from two-wire cables. (See circuit map 4, page 22.) Tuck wires into box, attach switches, receptacle, and coverplate.

Circuit #3
A 50-amp, 120/240-volt circuit serving the range.

- 50-amp receptacle for range
- 50-amp double-pole circuit breaker (see pages 58 to 59 for instructions on making final connections in the breaker panel)

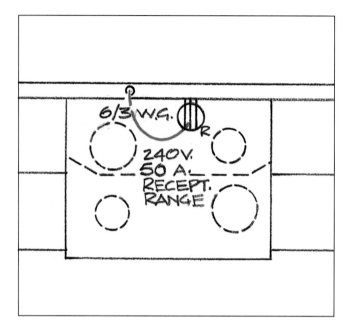

How to Install 120/240 Range Receptacle

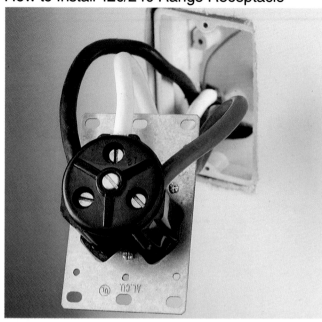

Attach the white wire to the neutral terminal, and the black and red wires to the remaining terminals. The neutral white wire acts as the grounding wire for this circuit, so push the bare copper ground wire from the cable to the back of the box. Tuck rest of the wires into the box. Attach receptacle and coverplate. (See circuit map 14, page 27.)

Circuit #4
A 20-amp, 120-volt circuit for the microwave.

- 20-amp duplex receptacle
- 20-amp single-pole circuit breaker (see pages 58 to 59 for instructions on making final connections in the breaker panel)

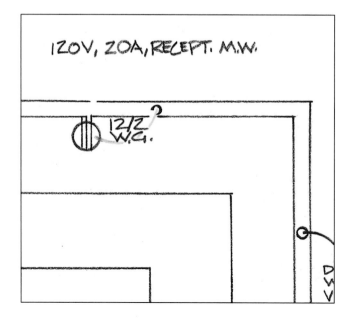

How to Connect Microwave Receptacle

Connect black wire from the cable to a brass screw terminal on the receptacle. Attach the white wire to a silver screw terminal, and the grounding wire to the receptacle's grounding screw. Tuck wires into box, attach the receptacle and the coverplate. (See circuit map 1, page 21.)

■ Circuit #5
A 15-amp, 120-volt circuit for the food disposer.

- 15-amp duplex receptacle
- Single-pole switch
- 15-amp single-pole circuit breaker (see pages 58 to 59 for instructions on making final connections in the breaker panel)

Note: Final connection of the single-pole switch controlling the disposer is shown on page 101.

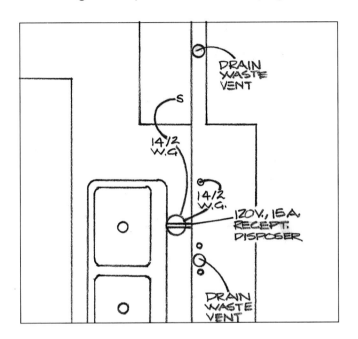

How to Connect Disposer Receptacle

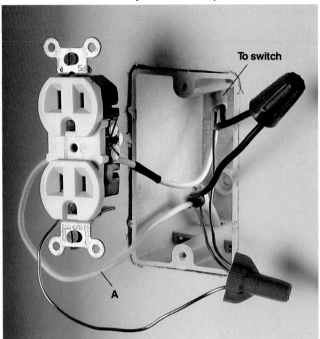

Connect black wires together. Connect white wire from feed cable (A) to silver screw on receptacle. Connect white wire from cable going to the switch to a brass screw terminal on the receptacle, and tag the wire with black indicating it is hot. Attach a grounding pigtail to grounding screw and to both cable grounding wires. Tuck wires into box, then attach receptacle and coverplate. (See circuit map 5, page 23.)

■ Circuit #6
A 15-amp, 120-volt circuit for the dishwasher.

- 15-amp duplex receptacle
- 15-amp single-pole circuit breaker (see pages 58 to 59 for instructions on making final connections in the breaker panel)

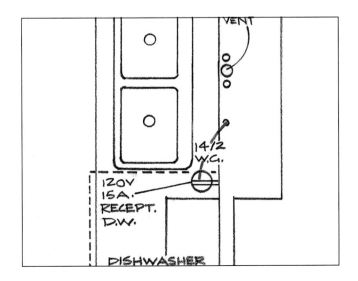

How to Connect Dishwasher Receptacle

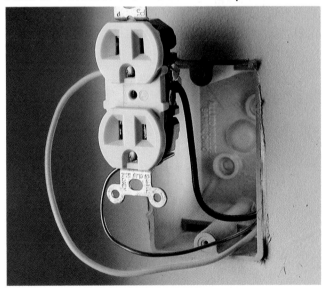

Connect the black wire to a brass screw terminal. Attach the white wire to a silver screw terminal. Connect the grounding wire to the grounding screw. Tuck wires into box, then attach receptacle and coverplate. (See circuit map 1, page 21.)

■ Circuit #7

A 15-amp basic lighting circuit serving the kitchen.

- 2 three-way switches with grounding screws
- 2 single-pole switches with grounding screws
- Ceiling light fixture
- 6 recessed light fixtures
- 4 fluorescent under-cabinet fixtures
- 15-amp single-pole circuit breaker (pages 58 to 59)

Note: Final connections for the single-pole switches are shown on page 101.

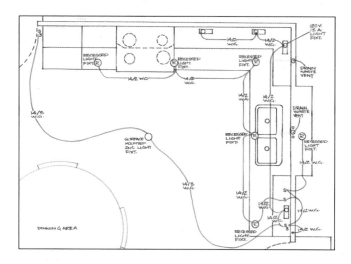

How to Connect First Three-way Switch

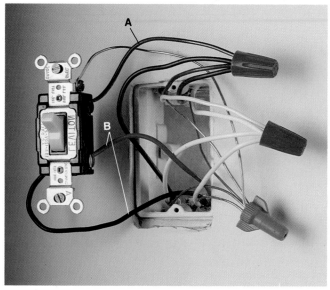

Connect a black pigtail to the common screw on the switch (A) and to the black wires from the two-wire cable. Connect black and red wires from the three-wire cable to traveler terminals (B) on the switch. Connect white wires from all cables entering box together. Attach a grounding pigtail to switch grounding screw and to all grounding wires in box. Tuck wires into box, then attach switch and coverplate. (See circuit map 17, page 29.)

How to Connect Surface-mounted Ceiling Fixture

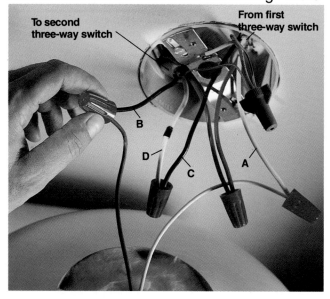

Connect white fixture lead to white wire (A) from first three-way switch. Connect black fixture lead to black wire (B) from second three-way switch. Connect black wire (C) from first switch to white wire (D) from second switch, and tag this white wire with black. Connect red wires from both switches together. Connect all grounding wires together. Mount fixture following manufacturer's instructions. (See circuit map 17, page 29.)

How to Connect Second Three-way Switch

Connect black wire from the cable to the common screw terminal (A). Connect red wire to one traveler screw terminal. Attach the white wire to the other traveler screw terminal and tag it with black, indicating it is hot. Attach the grounding wire to the grounding screw on the switch. Tuck wires in box, then attach switch and coverplate. (See circuit map 17, page 29.)

How to Connect Recessed Light Fixtures

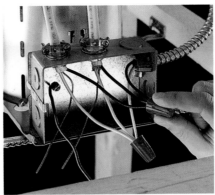

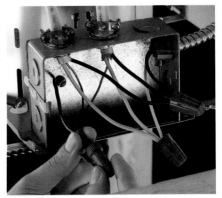

1 Make connections before installing wallboard: the work must be inspected first and access to the junction box is easier. Connect white cable wires to white fixture lead.

2 Connect black wires to black lead from fixture.

3 Attach a grounding pigtail to the grounding screw on the fixture, then connect all grounding wires. Tuck wires into the junction box, and replace the cover.

How to Connect Under-cabinet Fluorescent Task Light Fixtures

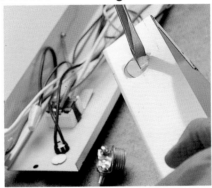

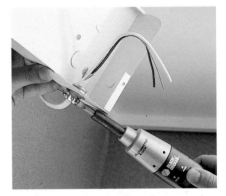

1 Drill 5/8" holes through wall and cabinet at locations that line up with knockouts on the fixture, and retrieve cable ends (page 97).

2 Remove access cover on fixture. Open one knockout for each cable that enters fixture box, and install cable clamps.

3 Strip 8" of sheathing from each cable end. Insert each end through a cable clamp, leaving 1/4" of sheathing in fixture box.

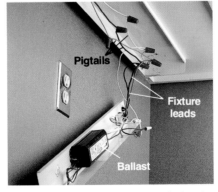

4 Screw fixture box to cabinet. Attach black, white, and green pigtails of THHN/THWN wire (page 42) to wires from one cable entering box. Pigtails must be long enough to reach the cable at other end of box.

5 Connect black pigtail and circuit wire to black lead from fixture. Connect white pigtail and circuit wire to white lead from fixture. Attach green pigtail and copper circuit wire to green grounding wire attached to the fixture box.

6 Tuck wires into box, and route THHN/THWN pigtails along one side of the ballast. Replace access cover and fixture lens.

Make hookups at circuit breaker panel (page 58) and arrange for the final inspection.

Installing Outdoor Wiring

Adding an outdoor circuit improves the value of your property and lets you enjoy your yard more fully. Doing the work yourself is also a good way to save money. Most outdoor wiring projects require digging underground trenches, and an electrician may charge several hundred dollars for this simple but time-consuming work.

Do not install your own wiring for a hot tub, fountain, or swimming pool. These outdoor water fixtures require special grounding techniques that are best left to an electrician.

In this chapter you learn how to install the following fixtures:

Decorative light fixtures (A) can highlight attractive features of your home and yard, like a deck, ornamental shrubs and trees, and flower gardens. See page 125.

A weatherproof switch (B) lets you control outdoor lights without going indoors. See page 122.

GFCI-protected receptacles (C) let you use electric lawn and garden tools, and provide a place to plug in radios, barbecue rotisseries, and other devices that help make your yard more enjoyable. See page 124.

A manual override switch (D) lets you control a motion-sensor light fixture from inside the house. See page 122.

Five Steps for Installing Outdoor Wiring

1. Plan the circuit (pages 112 to 113).
2. Dig trenches (pages 114 to 115).
3. Install boxes and conduit (pages 116 to 119).
4. Install UF cable (pages 120 to 121).
5. Make final connections (pages 122 to 125).

A motion-sensor light fixture (photos, right) provides inexpensive and effective protection against intruders. It has an infrared eye that triggers the light fixture when a moving object crosses its path. Choose a light fixture with a photo cell (E) that prevents the fixture from triggering in daylight. Look for an adjustable timer (F) that controls how long the light keeps shining after motion stops. Better models have range controls (G) to adjust the sensitivity of the motion-sensor eye. See page 122 to 123.

Installing Outdoor Wiring:
Cutaway View

The outdoor circuit installation shown on the following pages gives step-by-step instructions for installing a simple outdoor circuit for light fixtures and receptacles. The materials and techniques also can be applied to other outdoor wiring projects, such as running a circuit to a garage workshop, or to a detached shed or gazebo.

Your outdoor wiring probably will be different than the circuit shown in this chapter. Refer to the circuit maps on pages 20 to 31 as a guide for designing and installing your own outdoor electrical circuit.

Learn These Techniques for Installing Outdoor Wiring

A: Install weatherproof decorative light fixtures with watertight threaded fittings (page 125).

B: Use rigid metal or IMC conduit with threaded compression fittings (pages 118 to119) to protect exposed wires and cables.

C: Install a cast-aluminum switch box (page 121) to hold an outdoor switch. The box has a watertight coverplate with toggle lever built into it.

D: Use weatherproof receptacle boxes made of cast aluminum with sealed coverplates and threaded fittings to hold outdoor receptacles (pages 118 to 119).

E: Install a retrofit light fixture box (page 117) to hold a motion-sensor security light. Retrofit boxes are used to install electrical fixtures that fit inside existing finished walls. The box is sealed with a foam gasket that fits between the light fixture and the box.

F: Run NM cable (pages 48 to 49, 117) through walls to provide power to electrical boxes that fit inside finished walls.

G: Install retrofit single-gang boxes (page 117) to hold a manual override switch for the motion-sensor light, and the GFCI receptacle.

H: Attach a cast-aluminum extension ring to a retrofit receptacle box (page 118) to hold a GFCI receptacle.

I: Dig trenches (pages 114 to 115) to hold underground cables bringing power from the house to yard fixtures.

J: Install UF (underground feeder) cable (pages 120 to 121) to bring power from the house to the outdoor fixtures.

K: Run a feeder cable to connect the outdoor circuit to the circuit breaker panel (page 118).

Tools You Will Need:

Tape measure, drill with masonry bits and twist bits, jig saw or reciprocating saw, shovel, hammer, screwdriver, caulk gun, ball peen hammer or masonry hammer, masonry chisel, hacksaw, fish tape, cable ripper, combination tool, utility.knife, needlenose pliers.

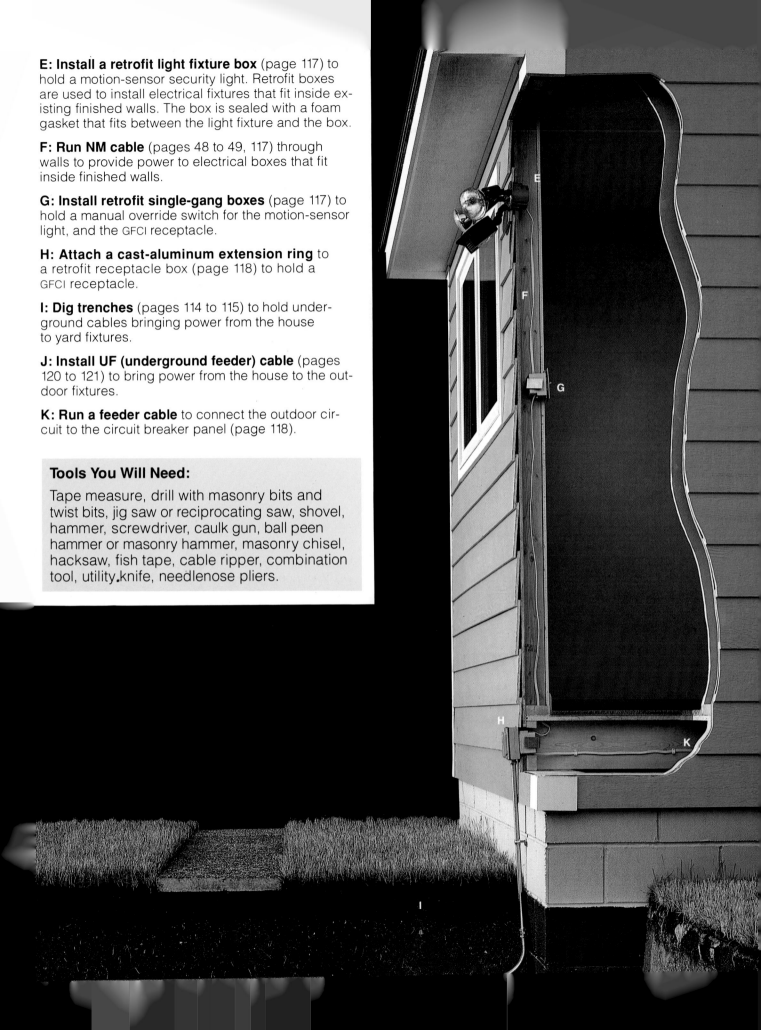

Installing Outdoor Wiring: Diagram View

This diagram view shows the layout of the outdoor wiring project featured on these pages. It includes the location of the switches, receptacles, light fixtures, and cable runs you will learn how to install in this chapter. The layout of your yard and the location of obstacles will determine the best locations for lights, receptacles, and underground cable runs. The wiring

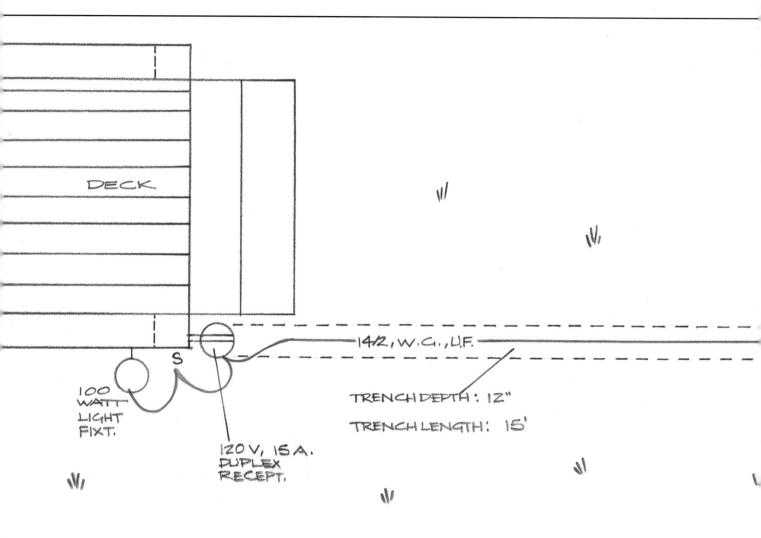

Yard is drawn to scale, with the lengths of trenches and cable runs clearly labeled.

Decorative light fixture is positioned to highlight the deck. Decorative fixtures should be used sparingly, to provide accent only to favorite features of your yard, such as flower beds, ornamental trees, or a patio.

Outdoor receptacle is positioned on the deck post, where it is accessible yet unobtrusive. Another good location for a receptacle is between shrubs.

diagram for your own project may differ greatly from the one shown here, but the techniques shown on the following pages will apply to any outdoor wiring project.

Note:
See pages 18 to 19 for a key to the common electrical symbols used in this diagram, and to learn how to draw your own wiring diagrams.

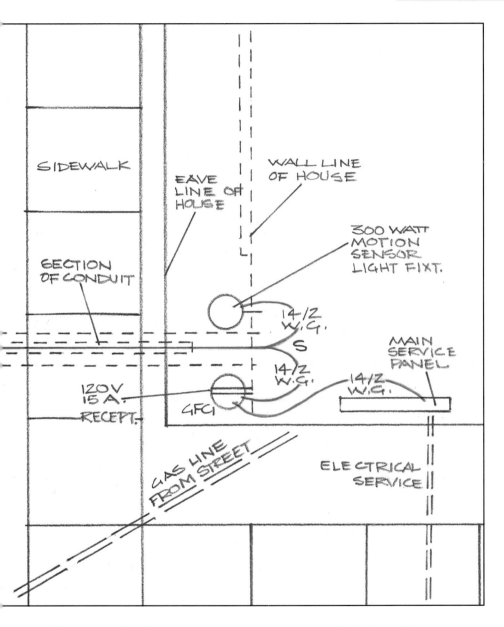

Motion-sensor security light is positioned so it has a good "view" of entryways to the yard and home, and is aimed so it will not shine into neighboring yards.

Manual override switch for motion-sensor light is installed at a convenient indoor location. Override switches are usually mounted near a door or window.

Entry point for circuit is chosen so there is easy access to the circuit breaker panel. Basement rim joists or garage walls make good entry points for an outdoor circuit.

Yard obstacles, like sidewalks and underground gas and electrical lines, are clearly marked as an aid to laying out cable runs.

Underground cables are laid out from the house to the outdoor fixtures by the shortest route possible to reduce the length of trenches.

GFCI receptacle is positioned near the start of the cable run, and is wired to protect all wires to the end of the circuit.

Check for underground utilities when planning trenches for underground cable runs. Avoid lawn sprinkler pipes; and consult your electric utility office, phone company, gas and water department, and cable television vendor for the exact locations of underground utility lines. Many utility companies send field representatives to show homeowners how to avoid dangerous underground hazards.

1: Plan the Circuit

As you begin planning an outdoor circuit, visit your electrical inspector to learn about local Code requirements for outdoor wiring. The techniques for installing outdoor circuits are much the same as for installing indoor wiring. However, because outdoor wiring is exposed to the elements, it requires the use of special weatherproof materials, including UF cable (page 42), rigid metal or schedule 40 PVC plastic conduit (pages 50 to 51), and weatherproof electrical boxes and fittings (pages 36 to 37).

The National Electrical Code (NEC) gives minimum standards for outdoor wiring materials, but because climate and soil conditions vary from region to region, your local Building and Electrical Codes may have more restrictive requirements. For example, some regions require that all underground cables be protected with conduit, even though the National Electrical Code allows UF cable to be buried without protection at the proper depths (page opposite).

For most homes, an outdoor circuit is a modest power user. Adding a new 15-amp, 120-volt circuit provides enough power for most outdoor electrical needs. However, if your circuit will include more than three large light fixtures (each rated for 300 watts or more) or more than four receptacles, plan to install a 20-amp, 120-volt circuit. Or, if your outdoor circuit will supply power to heating appliances or large workshop tools in a detached garage, you may require several 120-volt and 240-volt circuits.

Before drawing wiring plans and applying for a work permit, evaluate electrical loads (pages 14 to 17) to make sure the main service provides enough amps to support the added demand of the new wiring.

A typical outdoor circuit takes one or two weekends to install, but if your layout requires very long underground cables, allow yourself more time for digging trenches, or arrange to have extra help. Also make sure to allow time for the required inspection visits when planning your wiring project. See pages 6 to 13 for more information on planning a wiring project.

Choosing Cable Sizes for an Outdoor Circuit

Circuit Length		Circuit size
Less than 50 ft.	50 ft. or more	
14-gauge	12-gauge	15-amp
12-gauge	10-gauge	20-amp

Consider the circuit length when choosing cable sizes for an outdoor circuit. In very long circuits, normal wire resistance leads to a substantial drop in voltage. If your outdoor circuit extends more than 50 ft., use larger-gauge wire to reduce the voltage drop. For example, a 15-amp circuit that extends more than 50 ft. should be wired with 12-gauge wire instead of 14-gauge. A 20-amp circuit longer than 50 ft. should be wired with 10-gauge cable.

Tips for Planning an Outdoor Circuit

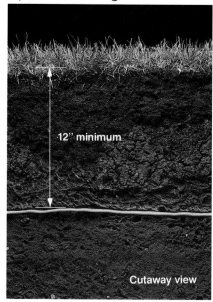

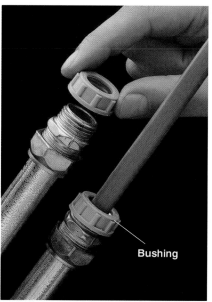

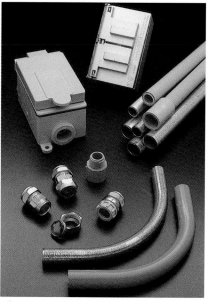

Bury UF cables 12" deep if the wires are protected by a GFCI and the circuit is no larger than 20 amps. Bury cable at least 18" deep if the circuit is not protected by a GFCI, or if it is larger than 20 amps.

Protect cable entering conduit by attaching a plastic bushing to the open end of the conduit. The bushing prevents sharp metal edges from damaging the vinyl sheathing on the cable.

Protect exposed wiring above ground level with rigid conduit and weatherproof electrical boxes and coverplates. Check your local Code restrictions: some regions allow the use of either rigid metal conduit or schedule 40 PVC plastic conduit and electrical boxes, while other regions allow only metal.

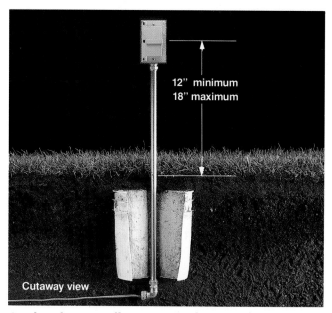

Prevent shock by making sure all outdoor receptacles are protected by GFCIs (page 10). A single GFCI receptacle can be wired to protect other fixtures on the circuit. Outdoor receptacles should be at least 1 ft. above ground level, and enclosed in weatherproof electrical boxes with watertight covers.

Anchor freestanding receptacles that are not attached to a structure by embedding the rigid metal conduit or schedule 40 PVC plastic conduit in a concrete footing. One way to do this is by running conduit through a plastic bucket, then filling the bucket with concrete. Freestanding receptacles should be at least 12", but no more than 18", above ground level—requirements vary, so check with your local inspector.

2: Dig Trenches

When laying underground cables, save time and minimize lawn damage by digging trenches as narrow as possible. Plan the circuit to reduce the length of cable runs.

If your soil is sandy, or very hard and dry, water the ground thoroughly before you begin digging. Lawn sod can be removed, set on strips of plastic, and replaced after cables are laid. Keep the removed sod moist but not wet, and replace it within two or three days. Otherwise, the grass underneath the plastic may die.

If trenches must be left unattended, make sure to cover them with scrap pieces of plywood to prevent accidents and to keep water out.

Materials You Will Need:

Stakes, string, plastic, scrap piece of conduit, compression fittings, plastic bushings.

How to Dig Trenches for Underground Cables

1 Mark the outline of trenches with wooden stakes and string.

2 Cut two 18"-wide strips of plastic, and place one strip on each side of the trench outline.

3 Remove blocks of sod from the trench outline, using a shovel. Cut sod 2" to 3" deep to keep roots intact. Place the sod on one of the plastic strips, and keep it moist.

4 Dig the trenches to the depth required by your local Code. Heap the dirt onto the second strip of plastic.

5 To run cable under a sidewalk, cut a length of metal conduit about 1 ft. longer than width of sidewalk, then flatten one end of the conduit to form a sharp tip.

6 Drive the conduit through the soil under the sidewalk, using a ball peen or masonry hammer and a wood block to prevent damage to the pipe.

7 Cut off the ends of the conduit with a hacksaw, leaving about 2" of exposed conduit on each side. Underground cable will run through the conduit.

8 Attach a compression fitting and plastic bushing to each end of the conduit. The plastic fittings will prevent the sharp edges of the conduit from damaging the cable sheathing.

9 If trenches must be left unattended, temporarily cover them with scrap plywood to prevent accidents.

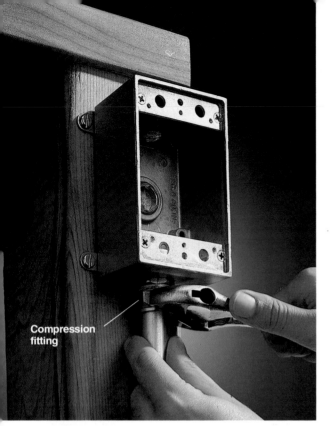

Compression fitting

Electrical boxes for an outdoor circuit must be weatherproof. This outdoor receptacle box made of cast aluminum has sealed seams, and is attached to conduit with threaded, watertight compression fittings.

3: Install Boxes & Conduit

Use cast-aluminum electrical boxes for outdoor fixtures and install metal conduit to protect any exposed cables, unless your Code has different requirements. Standard metal and plastic electrical boxes are not watertight, and should never be used outdoors. A few local Codes require you to install conduit to protect all underground cables, but in most regions this is not necessary. Some local Codes allow you to use boxes and conduit made with PVC plastic (pages 36 to 37).

Begin work by installing the retrofit boxes and the cables that run between them inside finished walls. Then install the outdoor boxes and conduit.

Materials You Will Need:

NM two-wire cable, cable staples, plastic retrofit light fixture box with grounding clip, plastic single-gang retrofit boxes with internal clamps, extension ring, silicone caulk, IMC or rigid metal conduit, pipe straps, conduit sweep, compression fittings, plastic bushings, Tapcon® anchors, single-gang outdoor boxes, galvanized screws, grounding pigtails, wire nuts.

How to Install Electrical Boxes & Conduit

1 Outline the GFCI receptacle box on the exterior wall. First drill pilot holes at the corners of the box outline, and use a piece of stiff wire to probe the wall for electrical wires or plumbing pipes. Complete the cutout with a jig saw or reciprocating saw.

Masonry variation: To make cutouts in masonry, drill a line of holes inside the box outline, using a masonry bit, then remove waste material with a masonry chisel and ball peen hammer.

2 From inside house, make the cutout for the indoor switch in the same stud cavity that contains the GFCI cutout. Outline the box on the wall, then drill a pilot hole and complete the cutout with a wallboard saw or jig saw.

3 On outside of house, make the cutout for the motion-sensor light fixture in the same stud cavity with the GFCI cutout. Outline the light fixture box on the wall, then drill a pilot hole and complete the cutout with a wallboard saw or jig saw.

4 Estimate the distance between the indoor switch box and the outdoor motion-sensor box, and cut a length of NM cable about 2 ft. longer than this distance. Use a fish tape to pull the cable from the switch box to the motion-sensor box. See pages 48 to 49 for tips on running cable through finished walls.

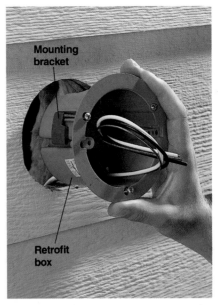

5 Strip about 10" of outer insulation from the end of the cable, using a cable ripper. Open a knockout in the retrofit light fixture box with a screwdriver. Insert the cable into the box so that at least 1/4" of outer sheathing reaches into the box.

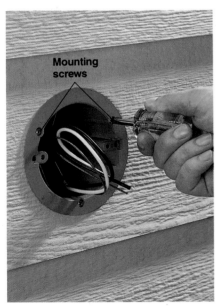

6 Insert the box into the cutout opening, and tighten the mounting screws until the brackets draw the outside flange firmly against the siding.

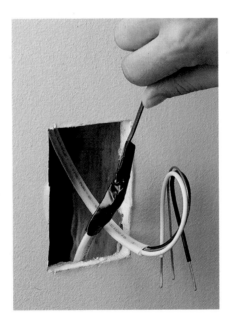

7 Estimate the distance between the outdoor GFCI cutout and the indoor switch cutout, and cut a length of NM cable about 2 ft. longer than this distance. Use a fish tape to pull the cable from the GFCI cutout to the switch cutout. Strip 10" of outer insulation from both ends of each cable.

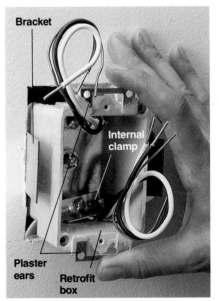

8 Open one knockout for each cable that will enter the box. Insert the cables so at least 1/4" of outer sheathing reaches inside box. Insert box into cutout, and tighten the mounting screw in the rear of the box until the bracket draws the plaster ears against the wall. Tighten internal cable clamps.

(continued next page)

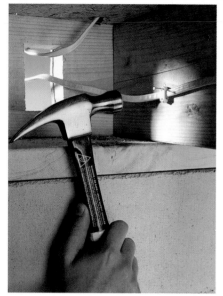

9 Install NM cable from circuit breaker panel to GFCI cutout. Allow an extra 2 ft. of cable at panel end, and an extra 1 ft. at GFCI end. Attach cable to framing members with cable staples. Strip 10" of outer sheathing from the GFCI end of cable, and 3/4" of insulation from each wire.

10 Open one knockout for each cable that will enter the GFCI box. Insert the cables so at least 1/4" of sheathing reaches into the box. Push the box into the cutout, and tighten the mounting screw until the bracket draws the plaster ears tight against the wall.

Foam gasket

Extension ring

11 Position a foam gasket over the GFCI box, then attach a extension ring to the box, using the mounting screws included with the extension ring. Seal any gaps around the extension ring with silicone caulk.

12 Measure and cut a length of IMC conduit to reach from the bottom of the extension ring to a point about 4" from the bottom of the trench. Attach the conduit to the extension ring using a compression fitting.

13 Anchor the conduit to the wall with a pipe strap and Tapcon® screws. Or, use masonry anchors and pan-head screws. Drill pilot holes for anchors, using a masonry drill bit.

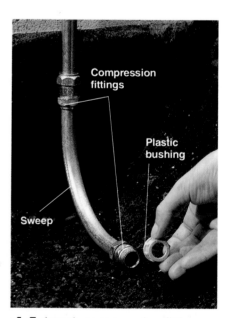

Compression fittings

Plastic bushing

Sweep

14 Attach compression fittings to the ends of metal sweep fitting, then attach the sweep fitting to the end of the conduit. Screw a plastic bushing onto the exposed fitting end of the sweep to keep the metal edges from damaging the cable.

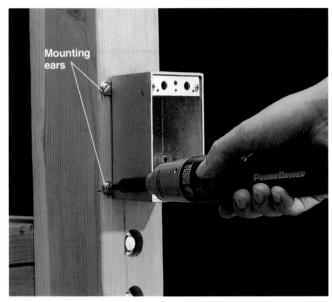

15 Attach mounting ears to the back of a weather-proof receptacle box, then attach the box to the deck frame by driving galvanized screws through the ears and into the post.

16 Measure and cut a length of IMC conduit to reach from the bottom of the receptacle box to a point about 4" from the bottom of the trench. Attach the conduit to the box with a compression fitting. Attach a sweep fitting and plastic bushing to the bottom of the conduit, using compression fittings (see step 14).

17 Cut a length of IMC conduit to reach from the top of the receptacle box to the switch box location. Attach the conduit to the receptacle box with a compression fitting. Anchor the conduit to the deck frame with pipe straps.

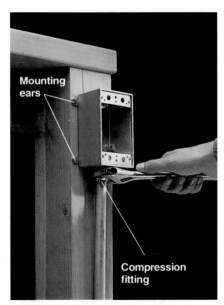

18 Attach mounting ears to the back of switch box, then loosely attach the box to the conduit with a compression fitting. Anchor the box to the deck frame by driving galvanized screws through the ears and into the wood. Then tighten the compression fitting with a wrench.

19 Measure and cut a short length of IMC conduit to reach from the top of the switch box to the deck light location. Attach the conduit with a compression fitting.

4: Install UF Cable

Use UF cable for outdoor wiring if the cable will come in direct contact with soil. UF cable has a solid-core vinyl sheathing, and cannot be stripped with a cable ripper. Instead, use a utility knife and the method shown (steps 5 & 6, page opposite). Never use NM cable for outdoor wiring. If your local Code requires that underground wires be protected by conduit, use THHN/THHW wire (page 42) instead of UF cable.

After installing all cables, you are ready for the rough-in inspection. While waiting for the inspector, temporarily attach the weatherproof coverplates to the boxes, or cover them with plastic to prevent moisture from entering. After the inspector has approved the rough-in work, fill in all cable trenches and replace the sod before making the final connections.

Materials You Will Need:

UF cable, electrical tape, grounding pigtails, wire nuts, weatherproof coverplates.

How to Install Outdoor Cable

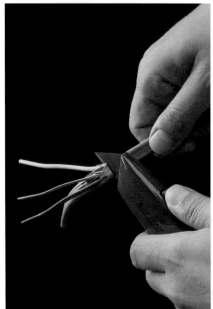

1 Measure and cut all UF cables, allowing an extra 12" at each box. At each end of the cable, use a utility knife to pare away about 3" of outer sheathing, leaving the inner wires exposed.

2 Feed a fish tape down through the conduit from the GFCI box. Hook the wires at one end of the cable through the loop in the fish tape, then wrap electrical tape around the wires up to the sheathing. Carefully pull the cable through the conduit.

3 Lay the cable along the bottom of the trench, making sure it is not twisted. Where cable runs under a sidewalk, use the fish tape to pull it through the conduit.

4 Use the fish tape to pull the end of the cable up through the conduit to the deck receptacle box at the opposite end of the trench. Remove the cable from the fish tape.

5 Cut away the electrical tape at each end of the cable, then clip away the bent wires. Bend back one of the wires in the cable, and grip it with needlenose pliers. Grip the cable with another pliers.

6 Pull back on the wire, splitting the sheathing and exposing about 10" of wire. Repeat with the remaining wires, then cut off excess sheathing with a utility knife. Strip 3/4" of insulation from the end of each wire, using a combination tool.

Switch box

7 Measure, cut, and install a cable from the deck receptacle box to the outdoor switch box, using the fish tape. Strip 10" of sheathing from each end of the cable, then strip 3/4" of insulation from the end of each wire, using a combination tool.

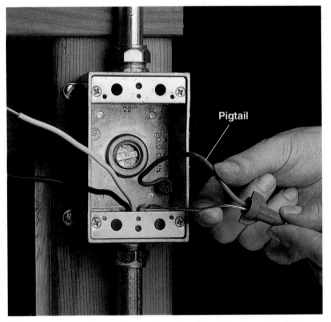

Pigtail

8 Attach a grounding pigtail to the back of each metal box and extension ring. Join all grounding wires with a wire nut. Tuck the wires inside the boxes, and temporarily attach the weatherproof coverplates until the inspector arrives for the rough-in inspection.

Arrange for the rough-in inspection before making the final connections.

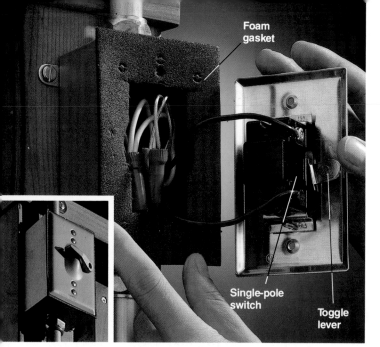

Foam
gasket

Single-pole
switch

Toggle
lever

Switches for outdoor use have weatherproof coverplates with built-in toggle levers. The lever operates a single-pole switch mounted to the inside of the coverplate. Connect the black circuit wire to one of the screw terminals on the switch, and connect the black wire lead from the light fixture to the other screw terminal. Use wire nuts to join the white circuit wires and the grounding wires. To connect the manual override switch for the motion-sensor light fixture, see circuit map 4 on page 22.

5: Make Final Connections

Make the final hookups for the switches, receptacles, and light fixtures after the rough-in cable installation has been reviewed and approved by your inspector, and after all trenches have been filled in. Install all the light fixtures, switches, and receptacles, then connect the circuit to the circuit breaker panel (pages 58 to 59).

Because outdoor wiring poses a greater shock hazard than indoor wiring, the GFCI receptacle (page 124) in this project is wired to provide shock protection for all fixtures controlled by the circuit.

When all work is completed and the outdoor circuit is connected at the service panel, your job is ready for final review by the inspector.

Materials You Will Need:

Motion-sensor light fixture, GFCI receptacle, 15-amp grounded receptacle, outdoor switch, decorative light fixture, wire nuts.

How to Connect a Motion-sensor Light Fixture

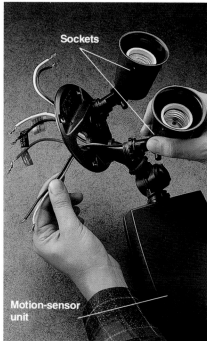

Sockets

Motion-sensor
unit

1 Assemble fixture by threading the wire leads from the motion-sensor unit and the bulb sockets through the faceplate knockouts. Screw the motion-sensor unit and bulb sockets into the faceplate.

Locknut

2 Secure the motion-sensor unit and the bulb sockets by tightening the locknuts.

Gasket

Fiber
washers

3 Insert the fiber washers into the sockets, and fit a rubber gasket over the end of each socket. The washers and gaskets ensure that the fixture will be watertight.

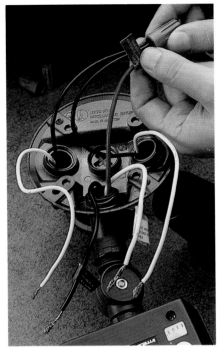 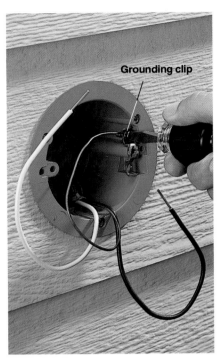 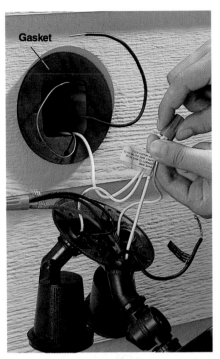

4 Connect the red wire lead from the motion-sensor unit to the black wire leads from the bulb sockets, using a wire nut. Some light fixtures have pre-tagged wire leads for easy installation.

5 Attach the bare copper grounding wire to the grounding clip on the box.

6 Slide the foam gasket over the circuit wires at the electrical box. Connect the white circuit wire to the white wire leads on the light fixture, using a wire nut.

7 Connect the black circuit wire to the black wire lead on the light fixture, using a wire nut.

8 Carefully tuck the wires into the box, then position the light fixture and attach the faceplate to the box, using the mounting screws included with the light fixture. (See also circuit map 4, page 22.)

How to Connect the GFCI Receptacle

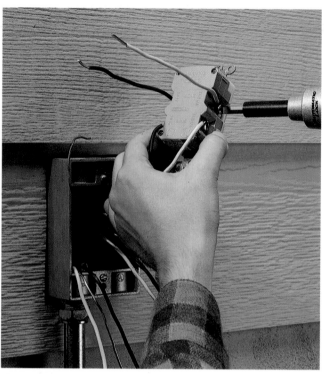

1 Connect the black feed wire from the power source to the brass terminal marked LINE. Connect the white feed wire from the power source to the silver screw terminal marked LINE.

2 Attach a short white pigtail wire to the silver screw terminal marked LOAD, and attach a short black pigtail wire to the brass screw terminal marked LOAD.

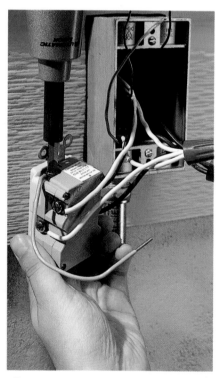

3 Connect the black pigtail wire to all the remaining black circuit wires, using a wire nut. Connect the white pigtail wire to the remaining white circuit wires.

4 Attach a grounding pigtail to the grounding screw on the GFCI. Join the grounding pigtail to the bare copper grounding wires, using a wire nut.

5 Carefully tuck wires into box. Mount GFCI, then fit a foam gasket over the box and attach the weatherproof coverplate. (See also circuit map 3, page 22.)

How to Connect an Outdoor Receptacle

1 Connect the black circuit wires to the brass screw terminals on the receptacle. Connect the white circuit wires to the silver screw terminals on the receptacle. Attach a grounding pigtail to the grounding screw on the receptacle, then join all grounding wires with a wire nut.

2 Carefully tuck all wires into the box, and attach the receptacle to the box, using the mounting screws. Fit a foam gasket over the box, and attach the weatherproof coverplate. (See also circuit map 1, page 21.)

How to Connect a Decorative Light Fixture

Compression fitting

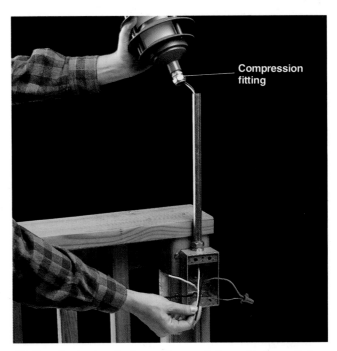

Compression fitting

1 Thread the wire leads of the light fixture through a threaded compression fitting. Screw the union onto the base of the light fixture.

2 Feed wire leads through conduit and into switch box. Slide light fixture onto conduit, and tighten compression fitting. Connect black wire lead to one screw terminal on switch, and connect white wire lead to white circuit wire. (See also circuit map 4, page 22.)

Make hookups at circuit breaker panel (page 58) and arrange for final inspection.

INDEX

For Product Information:

If you have difficulty finding any of
the following materials featured in this
book, call the manufacturer and ask for
the name of the nearest sales representative. The representative will direct
you to retailers that sell the product in
your area.

Blower-heater (page 73)
  Nautilus (Fan-forced wall heater)
  Telephone: 1-800-637-1453

Ceiling fan brace bar (page 75)
  Reiker Enterprises Inc. (Easy Brace)
  Telephone: 1-205-820-1520

Deck light (page 106)
  L. E. Mason Co.
  Telephone: 1-617-361-1710

Motion-sensor light fixture (page 107)
  Intellectron (Model BC9000K)
  Telephone: 1-800-828-9887

Stack-It® Cable Staples (page 43)
  3-M Electrical Products Div.
  Telephone: 1-800-245-3573

Sonic measuring tools (page 10)
  Cooper Tools (Lufkin® ultrasonic tool)
  Telephone: 919-362-7510
  Sonin Inc. (ultrasonic measuring tool)
  Telephone: 1-800-223-7511

Telephone & TV outlets (pages 78-79)
  Gemini Industries (signal splitter,
    cable wall plate)
  Telephone: 1-800-526-7452

Creative Publishing international, Inc. offers
a variety of how-to books.
For information write:
  Creative Publishing international, Inc.
  Subscriber Books
  5900 Green Oak Drive
  Minnetonka, MN 55343